COELIAC DISEASE

The Essential Guide

Need
— 2 —
Know

Kate
Coxon

D0258475

First published in Great Britain in 2010 by
Need2Know
Remus House
Coltsfoot Drive
Peterborough
PE2 9JX
Telephone 01733 898103
Fax 01733 313524
www.need2knowbooks.co.uk

Need2Know is an imprint of Forward Press Ltd.
www.forwardpress.co.uk
SB ISBN 978-1-86144-087-7
Cover photograph: Dreamstime

Contents

Introduction

When you're diagnosed with coeliac disease, the questions can seem overwhelming. What can I eat? What can't I eat? Why do I have to avoid gluten? How do I tell people about my condition? What about cooking, shopping and eating out?

It's thought that around 1 in 100 people has coeliac disease, although many remain undiagnosed. Gluten is a protein found in wheat, rye and barley, and when a person with coeliac disease eats gluten it triggers an immune reaction which damages the gut. Some people with coeliac disease may also be sensitive to oats.

Thankfully, the treatment for coeliac disease is straightforward: people diagnosed with the condition must avoid gluten in their diet. However, eating is something that we need to do three times a day, seven days a week, 365 days a year. Being diagnosed with coeliac disease can mean changing your eating, cooking and shopping habits for good.

The good news is that unlike many other conditions, there is no medication to take. If you stick to a gluten-free diet, you can stay healthy. Once you've got the hang of it, the diet may be easier to manage than you think. Many foods are naturally gluten free, and most supermarkets now have a 'free from' section where you can buy a wide range of gluten-free, substitute products. Improvements to the food labelling system in recent years mean that it's now much easier to identify which products contain gluten and which are safe for you to eat. There's no denying that following a gluten-free diet is a major undertaking, and you may need support.

Perhaps you've just been diagnosed with coeliac disease, or you have a child, friend or relative who has. Maybe you're looking for more information on coeliac disease, or think that you or another family member might have the condition. Whatever your situation, this essential guide will take you through the basics of the condition, from symptoms and diagnosis, to getting started on your gluten-free diet and sticking to it. It will show you how to manage your diet, how to get the most from your prescription and how to stay healthy, offering practical advice to help you cope with everyday tasks such as shopping, cooking, eating out, travel and holidays. It also covers some of the issues facing children and teenagers with coeliac disease and includes many tips for gluten-free living at home as well as on the move. There's information on some of the related health conditions you'll need to know about, as well as the follow-up care you can expect from your healthcare team.

There are many myths about coeliac disease and it may sometimes feel like a complicated condition. By contrast, the treatment is very simple: you need to follow a gluten-free diet. With the help of this guide, making the switch to a gluten-free lifestyle can be a straightforward process. Being diagnosed with coeliac disease doesn't have to mean the end to good food: it can be the start of a healthy and enjoyable new way of eating.

Acknowledgements

My main source of information in researching and writing this book has been Coeliac UK, the charity that supports people with the condition. I would like to thank everyone at Coeliac UK for their help and support, and in particular Nicola Crawford-Taylor.

Coeliac UK has been an invaluable resource for my whole family since my children were diagnosed with coeliac disease in 2005. I would urge anyone with coeliac disease, or anyone who has a child with the condition, to join Coeliac UK.

Disclaimer

This book is for general information on coeliac disease only and is not intended to replace professional medical advice. The author cannot be held responsible for claims arising from the inappropriate use of any dietary regime. Please consult your GP before changing, stopping or starting any medical treatment. The author and publishers disclaim, as far as the law allows, any liability arising directly or indirectly from the use or misuse of the information contained in this book.

Chapter One

What is Coeliac Disease?

Many people think coeliac disease (pronounced 'see-liac') is an allergy or a simple food intolerance. In fact, it's an autoimmune disease, where the body's immune system attacks its own tissues. In people with coeliac disease, this immune reaction is triggered by gluten.

Gluten is the collective name for a type of protein found in the cereals wheat, rye and barley. A small number of people are also sensitive to oats.

When a person with coeliac disease eats gluten, the lining of the gut (the small intestine, also known as the small bowel) becomes damaged. Tiny, finger-like projections in the small intestine called 'villi' become inflamed and flattened. This leaves a smaller surface area to absorb nutrients and as a result, people with undiagnosed coeliac disease often have nutritional deficiencies, as well as a wide range of symptoms, including gut problems.

> 'Gluten is the collective name for a type of protein found in the cereals wheat, rye and barley. A small number of people are also sensitive to oats.'

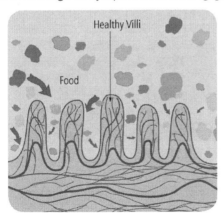

Healthy villi are shown on the left. On the right is damage to the villi in someone with untreated coeliac disease.

© Coeliac UK.

What are the symptoms of coeliac disease?

The symptoms of coeliac disease can range from mild to severe and will vary from person to person.

Possible symptoms include:

- Bloating, abdominal pain, nausea, diarrhoea, excessive wind, heartburn, indigestion, constipation.
- Any combination of iron, vitamin B12 or folic acid deficiency.
- Tiredness, headaches.
- Weight loss (but not in all cases).
- Recurrent mouth ulcers.
- Hair loss (alopecia).
- Skin rash (dermatitis herpetiformis).
- Defective tooth enamel.
- Osteoporosis.
- Depression.
- Infertility.
- Recurrent miscarriages.
- Joint or bone pain.
- Neurological (nerve) problems such as ataxia (poor muscle co-ordination) and neuropathy (numbness and tingling in the hands and feet).

Sometimes symptoms can be confused with irritable bowel syndrome (IBS) or wheat intolerance, while others may be put down to stress or even getting older.

Contrary to popular belief, you don't need to be underweight or to have lost weight to have coeliac disease. Often when a diagnosis is made, people are of normal weight or may even be overweight.

In babies, gut symptoms may develop after weaning onto gluten cereals. Symptoms in young children include a bloated tummy and irritability accompanied by muscle wasting in the arms and legs. Some infants may gradually fail to gain weight, or may lose weight. In older children, symptoms vary as they do in adults. Poor growth, short stature, anaemia (iron deficiency) and recurrent mouth ulcers are some of the symptoms of coeliac disease in children.

Why do I have to follow a gluten-free diet?

We know that people with coeliac disease react to gluten, and that eating gluten triggers the immune response that damages the gut.

The good news for people with coeliac disease is that when gluten is removed from the diet, the source of their problems is also removed. Although it may take some time for the gut to heal, if a person with coeliac disease continues to avoid gluten, their symptoms will improve. The gut eventually repairs itself and its ability to absorb food returns to normal. Thankfully, the health risks associated with coeliac disease are minimised as long as people with the condition stick to a gluten-free diet.

Which foods can I eat?

It can be helpful to think in terms of three main food groups:

- Foods that are naturally gluten free, which you can eat freely.
- Gluten-free substitute products.
- Some processed food such as soups or baked beans provided they do not have gluten-containing cereals as an ingredient.

Foods that are naturally gluten free include:

- Potatoes, all types of rice and corn (also called maize).
- Breakfast cereals made from rice and corn.
- Plain meat, fish and chicken.
- Pulses, such as beans, peas and lentils.

- Polenta, quinoa and millet.
- Eggs, milk, cheese and most yoghurts.
- Fruits and juices.
- Vegetables.

Which foods contain gluten?

You will need to avoid gluten-containing cereals such as:

- Wheat (including spelt, couscous, semolina, bulgar wheat and kamut).
- Rye.
- Barley.
- 'Cross breeds' of these cereals (e.g. triticale).

The most obvious sources of gluten are breads, cereals, pastas, flours, pizza bases, cakes and biscuits. Gluten-containing cereals can also be used as an ingredient of soups, sauces, ready meals and processed food such as sausages.

However, remember that you will still be able to buy or make your own gluten-free substitutes that will be safe for you to eat. More information on what you can and what you can't eat is given in chapter 2.

How common is coeliac disease?

It's thought that around 1 in 100 people are affected with coeliac disease, although many of these are undiagnosed. National Institute for Clinical Excellence (NICE) guidelines suggest only about 10-15% of people with coeliac disease are clinically diagnosed. Because the symptoms vary in severity from person to person and can affect different parts of the body, it can take an average of 13 years to get diagnosed with the condition. Many people who are eventually diagnosed with the condition feel in some way 'lucky' that the cause of their symptoms has been discovered, particularly if they have felt unwell for a long time.

Does coeliac disease run in families?

Coeliac disease is an autoimmune disease that appears in people who have the genes that predispose them to develop it. Evidence suggests that there is an increased risk of 1 in 10 when coeliac disease exists in a family, so if you have a first-degree relative (e.g. father, mother, son or daughter) with coeliac disease, you'll need to be extra vigilant about developing the condition. But coeliac disease is not 'catching'!

How is coeliac disease diagnosed?

For anyone who thinks they may have coeliac disease, it's essential to continue to eat gluten until tests and investigations are done, in order to make a definite diagnosis.

There are three steps in the diagnosis:

1. Discuss your symptoms with your GP.

2. Your GP will take a simple blood test. A coeliac disease blood test looks for a type of antibody that the body makes in response to eating gluten. The most accurate blood tests for coeliac disease detect the following antibodies:

- Tissue transglutaminase antibody (tTGA).
- Endomysial antibody (EMA).

The laboratory performing the test may measure one of these antibodies, or sometimes both.

If the blood test is positive, your GP should move to step 3. However, a few people with coeliac disease do not make these antibodies. Therefore, people with 'strongly suggestive' symptoms of coeliac disease and/or people who have a close relative with the condition, could talk to their GP about moving to step 3, despite having a negative blood test.

3. Your GP will refer you to a gastroenterologist (specialist gut doctor) for a simple test called a gut biopsy. A thin flexible tube called an endoscope is passed via your mouth and stomach into the small intestine. Small samples of gut lining (biopsies) are collected and later examined under a microscope to check for abnormalities that are typical in coeliac disease.

This is normally done using a local anaesthetic spray that numbs the back of the throat, or with a sedative given by injection. In children, the biopsies are usually performed under a general anaesthetic.

These tests are recommended to confirm a diagnosis of coeliac disease in both adults and children. If you have any concerns about these tests, the best thing to do is to discuss it with your healthcare team.

When steps 1-3 have been completed, depending on the results, a medical diagnosis of coeliac disease may be given.

'It's very important to have a medical confirmation of coeliac disease for a number of reasons.'

Why is a medical diagnosis important?

It's very important to have a medical confirmation of coeliac disease for a number of reasons. First, the symptoms of coeliac disease can be similar to other medical conditions, so it's vital to make sure that coeliac disease is indeed the cause of those symptoms and not another medical condition. It's important that people with coeliac disease get the necessary support and review from their healthcare team. A lifelong gluten-free diet is a major undertaking, which has an impact on food choice and variety. People with coeliac disease will need advice, support and monitoring to ensure their diet is gluten free, and provides enough nutrients to promote long-term health. Children will need their growth and development checked on a regular basis.

If you are medically diagnosed with coeliac disease, you can receive prescriptions for gluten-free substitute products from your GP, which can help you maintain your diet and can also help supplement the cost of these products.

Are there any alternative tests for coeliac disease?

Alternative tests that claim to diagnose food-related 'problems or intolerances' (such as hair analysis, applied kinesiology or any other tests) are not regarded as accurate and do not diagnose coeliac disease.

The only recognised and accurate way to be tested is by contacting your GP and working through steps 1-3.

I think I might have coeliac disease – what should I do?

If you think you may have coeliac disease, you should continue to eat gluten and follow steps 1-3 above. It is very important that you do not remove gluten from your diet at this stage. The tests for coeliac disease work because they look at how the body is responding to eating gluten, so if you're not eating gluten, or if you reduce the amount of gluten you eat before being tested, you may cause a 'false negative' result for both the blood test and the gut biopsy.

If you've cut gluten out of your diet, you'll need to reintroduce it before getting tested to make sure the tests for coeliac disease are meaningful.

How much gluten should I eat to get tested?

The reaction to eating gluten varies from person to person, and it's difficult to say exactly how much gluten is needed.

Guidelines produced by NICE in 2009 recommend that you should eat some gluten (for example, bread, chapattis, pasta, biscuits or cakes) in more than one meal every day for a minimum of six weeks before testing.

Summing Up

- Coeliac disease is an autoimmune disease and gluten is the trigger.
- Gluten is a protein found in wheat, rye and barley; a few people are also sensitive to oats.
- Symptoms vary from person to person.
- A gluten-free diet is the only treatment for coeliac disease.
- Medical diagnosis is by blood test and gut biopsy.
- You must not stop eating gluten until tests for coeliac disease are complete.

Chapter Two

Going Gluten Free

What happens once I have been diagnosed?

Once your diagnosis is complete, you need to start a gluten-free diet. This is currently the only treatment for coeliac disease. The process of gut healing begins as soon as gluten is removed from your diet, and you will probably start to feel better within a few weeks. However, it can take time – anything from six months up to two years or more – for the gut to fully recover.

Accepting the diagnosis

You may feel relieved when you are finally told that you have coeliac disease, particularly if you have felt unwell or had symptoms for a long while. If it has taken a long time for the condition to be diagnosed, you may feel angry or frustrated. Being told that you have a lifelong condition can make some people feel depressed, and this is understandable. Over time, and especially as you begin to feel better on a gluten-free diet, you may find it easier to accept the condition. Make sure that you discuss any concerns with your GP.

Join Coeliac UK

A good starting point is to join Coeliac UK, the national charity supporting people with the condition (see the help list). Coeliac UK will send you an information pack and they also have a helpline to answer any questions you have. You may find it helpful to talk to other people who have also been diagnosed with the condition. Coeliac UK can put you in touch with local groups so that you can get in contact with others in a similar situation.

Referral to a dietitian

Once you have been diagnosed, your GP or gastroenterologist should refer you to a dietitian. Consultations with a dietitian within the NHS are free and usually take place at your local hospital outpatient department, or at your GP surgery. The dietitian will be able to advise you on how to make changes to your diet so that you are no longer eating foods containing gluten. The dietitian may also have some suggestions about the kinds of foods that you can get on prescription (see chapter 4 for more information). You will also need to discuss prescriptions with your GP.

Getting the most out of your appointment with the dietitian

'Once you have been diagnosed with coeliac disease, your GP or gastroenterologist should refer you to a dietitian.'

Before your appointment with the dietitian, you may find it helpful to make a note of the kinds of food you normally eat over a two to three day period. One way of doing this is to keep a food diary for a few days. It's also a good idea to jot down any specific questions or concerns you have and write down a list of your likes and dislikes, which will be helpful in planning your diet. The dietitian should also give you written information about foods you can and can't eat, and talk to you about foods available on prescription. Make sure you ask for a follow-up appointment as it's important to see your dietitian regularly. They can keep you up to date with new information and products and ensure that you are getting a balanced diet.

If you are vegetarian or vegan, make sure to mention this to your dietitian so that they can take this into account when helping you to plan your diet.

When you are first diagnosed, it's possible that you may be deficient in important nutrients. The dietitian will be able to discuss any questions you have, including whether or not you should take any supplements.

What can/can't I eat?

The only treatment for coeliac disease is a gluten-free diet. The good news is that many foods are naturally gluten free and completely safe for people with coeliac disease to eat.

To recap, gluten is a protein that's found in the cereals wheat, rye and barley. As we saw in chapter 1, gluten is present in many foods, such as bread, biscuits, cakes and pastry (i.e. foods which are made from wheat, rye and barley flour). It can also be in other foods that you might not expect: for example, some sausages, sauces, ready meals and soups.

It may be helpful to think of food in these categories:

- Food that is safe to eat (this is food which is naturally gluten free).
- Food that you need to check (food which may or may not contain gluten).
- Food you must avoid (or replace with gluten-free substitutes).

The checklist below gives you more information about foods that are safe, as well as those that you need to check and avoid or replace.

Gluten free	Need to check	Not gluten free
Cereals and flour Corn, cornflour, rice, rice flour, arrowroot, amanth, buckwheat, millet, teff, quinoa, sorghum, soya flour, potato starch, modified starch, potato flour, gram flour, polenta (cornmeal), sago, tapioca, cassava, urd/urid flour, pure uncontaminated oats	**Cereals and flour** Flavoured, savoury rice products	**Cereals and flour** Wheat, bulgar wheat, durum wheat, wheat bran, wheat rusk, wheat starch, semolina, couscous, barley, barley malt, barley flour, rye, rye flour, triticale, kamut, spelt
Bread, cakes and biscuits Gluten-free breads, biscuits, cakes, pizza bases, rolls and flour mixes	**Bread, cakes and biscuits** Meringues, macaroons	**Bread, cakes and biscuits** All breads, chapattis, biscuits, crackers, cakes, pastries, scones, muffins, pizzas bases made from wheat, rye or barley flour
Pasta and noodles Corn pasta, rice pasta, gluten-free pasta, rice noodles	**Pasta and noodles**	**Pasta and noodles** Fresh, dried and canned wheat pasta, noodles

'The only treatment for coeliac disease is a gluten-free diet. The good news is that many foods are naturally gluten free and completely safe for people with coeliac disease to eat.'

Gluten free	Need to check	Not gluten free
Breakfast cereals Gluten-free muesli, buckwheat flakes	**Breakfast cereals** Malted breakfast cereals, porridge oats	**Breakfast cereals** Wheat-based breakfast cereals, muesli
Meat and poultry All fresh meats and poultry, smoked meats, cured pure meats, plain cooked meats	**Meat and poultry** Meat pastes, patés, sausages, burgers	**Meat and poultry** Meat and poultry cooked in batter or breadcrumbs, faggots, rissoles, haggis, breaded ham
Fish and shellfish All fresh fish and shellfish, smoked, kippered and dried fish, fish canned in oil or brine	**Fish and shellfish** Fish in sauce, fish pastes and patés	**Fish and shellfish** Fish in batter or breadcrumbs, fish cakes, taramasalata, fish fingers
Cheese and eggs All cheeses, eggs	**Cheese and eggs**	**Cheese and eggs** Scotch eggs
Milk and milk products All milk (liquid and dried), all cream (single, double, whipping, clotted, soured and crème frâiche), buttermilk, plain yoghurt, plain fromage frais	**Milk and milk products** Coffee and tea whiteners, oat milk, fruit and flavoured yoghurt/fromage frais, soya desserts	**Milk and milk products** Milk with added fibre, yoghurt and fromage frais containing muesli or cereals
Fats and oils Butter, margarine, lard, cooking oils, ghee, reduced and low fat spreads	**Fats and oils** Suet	**Fats and oils**
Fruit and vegetables All fresh, frozen, canned and dried pure fruits and vegetables. Vegetables pickled in vinegar, all peas including mushy, processed and marrowfat	**Fruit and vegetables** Fruit pie fillings Potato products – oven, microwave and frozen chips, instant mash, waffles	**Fruit and vegetables** Vegetables and potatoes in batter, breadcrumbs or dusted with flour, potato croquettes
Nuts, seeds and pulses All pulses (beans, peas and lentils), plain nuts and seeds	**Nuts, seeds and pulses** Dry roasted nuts	**Nuts, seeds and pulses**

Need2Know

Gluten free	Need to check	Not gluten free
Savoury snacks Homemade popcorn, rice cakes, rice crackers	**Savoury snacks** Plain potato or flavoured crisps	**Savoury snacks** Snacks made from wheat, rye, barley, pretzels
Preserves and spreads Sugar and glucose molasses, jam, conserves, honey, golden syrup, treacle, marmalade	**Preserves and spreads** Mincemeat, lemon curd, peanut and other nut butters	**Preserves and spreads**
Soups, sauces, pickles, and seasonings Tomato and garlic puree, individual herbs and spices, vinegars, mixed herbs and spices, ground pepper, mint sauces, Worcestershire sauce	**Soups, sauces, pickles, and seasonings** Gravy granules, stock cubes, canned or packet soups, packet and jarred sauces and mixes, tamari (Japanese soy sauce), mustard products, mayonnaise, salad cream, dressings, pickles and chutney, blended seasoning, curry powder	**Soups, sauces, pickles, and seasonings** Chinese soy sauce, stuffing mix
Confectionery and puddings Jelly, liquorice root, seaside rock	**Confectionery and puddings** Chocolates, ice-cream, mousses, liquorice sweets	**Confectionery and puddings** Puddings made using wheat flour and/or semolina
Drinks Tea, coffee, cocoa, fruit juice, squash, clear fizzy drinks, Complan™, Build up™, wine, spirits, cider, sherry, port, liqueurs, gluten-free beers	**Drinks** Drinking chocolate, cloudy fizzy drinks, vending machine hot chocolate	**Drinks** Malted milk drinks, barley waters/squash, beer, lager, ales, stouts
Miscellaneous Gelatine, bicarbonate of soda, cream of tartar, fresh and dried yeast, artificial sweeteners, Bovril™, Marmite™, icing sugars, yeast extract	**Miscellaneous** Tofu, cake decorations, marzipan, baking powder, ready to use icings	**Miscellaneous** Ice cream cones and wafers

© Coeliac UK, Gluten-free checklist.

Which grains are gluten free?

Along with the well-known grains or cereals such as wheat, there are many grains that you may not have heard of. Some of these, like quinoa or millet, are gluten free. Others, such as spelt and couscous, are not gluten free, and you'll need to avoid them. Coeliac UK has prepared a list of grains to help you choose safely.

Contains gluten
Barley – people with coeliac disease should avoid products containing barley and products high in malted barley, such as malted drinks, beers, ales, lagers and stouts. Barley malt extract – often used in small amounts as a flavour enhancer can be tolerated by most people when used at a low level. If you are unsure whether the level contained in a product is suitable or not, check your *Food and Drink Directory*, or contact the manufacturer directly. Bulgar wheat – made from wheat. Couscous – prepared from wheat. Durum wheat – wheat used in making pasta. Einkorn – form of wheat. Emmer – form of wheat. Kamut® – ancient relative of modern durum wheat. Pearl barley – barley which has been hulled and the bran removed, used in some soups. Rye – cereal cultivated for its grain – used for flour and rye bread. Semolina – coarse particles of wheat, used to make pasta and puddings and for coating roast potatoes. Spelt – ancient form of wheat. Triticale – a cross between wheat and rye. Wheat – used widely to make bread, pasta, biscuits and cakes.
Oats
Oats – contain gluten for food labelling purposes. Research suggests most people may tolerate pure, uncontaminated oats; however most oat/oat products on the market are contaminated with gluten, and therefore unsuitable. Check with your dietitian before eating pure, uncontaminated oats so they can monitor your symptoms. Pure, uncontaminated oat products are listed in Appendix III of the current edition of the *Food and Drink Directory.*

Gluten free

Agar – obtained from algae – can be used as an alternative to gelatine for making jellies and desserts.

Almond – often ground and used as an alternative to flour in bakery products.

Amaranth – a plant used to make cereal alternatives.

Besan – see Gram flour.

Buckwheat – used to make flour and noodles.

Carageenan – used as thickener, stabiliser, emulsifier.

Cassava/Manioc/Tapioca – plant/vegetable used as a cereal product. Tapioca is the beady starch extracted from the root of the cassava (manioc) – used for puddings or as a thickener.

Chana – see Gram flour.

Chestnut – ground and used as flour.

Corn – also called maize – a cereal used as a basis for flour/starch and other products.

Flax/Linseed – seeds can be added to muesli.

Gram flour/Garam flour – made from chickpeas, typically used in Indian cuisine.

Hemp – flour and seeds used in bakery products and muesli.

Hops – the flowers of a hardy vine plant used in the brewing of beer.

Maize – see corn.

Millet/Bajra – a cereal often used in gluten-free muesli.

Mustard – flour, powder, seeds and oil.

Polenta – made from boiled cornmeal.

Potato – can be used to thicken sauces and soups – flour/starch used in baking.

Pulses (peas, beans, lentils) – can be ground to produce flours, and can be used in a variety of dishes.

Quinoa – a pseudocereal – its seeds are used in muesli and baking.

Rice – all types, e.g. wild, arborio, aromatic, basmati, black and red.

Sago – powdery starch extracted from sago palms, can be used as thickener or cereal product.

Sesame – available as oil and seeds.

Sorghum – a grain which can be used as a source of syrup.

Soya – flour used in gluten-free bakery products.

Tapioca – see Cassava.

Teff – a grass with very small seeds – its flour can be used in baking.

Urd/Urid/Urad flour – made from lentils.

© Coeliac UK, A-Z of common plants, seeds, grains, cereals & flours.

Gluten-free 'substitute' food

Specialist gluten-free 'substitute' foods (gluten-free bread, gluten-free pasta, etc) are readily available and you can get these:

- On prescription from your GP (see chapter 4).
- In the 'free from' section in supermarkets.
- In health food shops.
- By mail order and Internet.

Coeliac UK publishes a magazine, called *Crossed Grain*, three times a year which is available when you join. Many food manufacturers advertise their products there as well as on the website. Coeliac UK's *Food and Drink Directory* lists manufacturers of specialist gluten-free food, some of these are listed in the help list at the end of this book.

How do I know which gluten-free food to choose?

Gluten-free specialist, or substitute, food is a market that has expanded rapidly in recent years. Most supermarkets now have a 'free from' section with a large range of products including their own brands as well as those made by specialist manufacturers.

The good news is that there is much greater choice available. The downside is that you may feel overwhelmed when you first look at the vast range on offer. This is where the advice and support of a dietitian is vital. Recommendations from other people with coeliac disease can also be helpful.

Over time you will get used to what you can and can't eat. You may need to try out different brands or types of food before you find ones that you like. Even within one basic food type (for example, gluten-free pasta) there is a lot of variety. A packet of gluten-free spaghetti made by one manufacturer may be very different in taste and texture to another brand of gluten-free spaghetti, and may take longer to cook. You may want to experiment a little, depending on the type of products you buy, where you do your shopping and your own individual likes or dislikes.

Contacting manufacturers for samples

One suggestion is to contact different manufacturers of specialist gluten-free foods and ask them if they have any free samples that they could send you. Many companies are happy to send you samples of food to try and some may even send you recipes. It's a good idea to try to 'stagger' this process though and only contact a few at a time, otherwise you may find you have a lot of food that needs to be eaten in a short space of time.

Who can advise me about my diet?

Dietitians can advise you about your diet. The *Food and Drink Directory* is also a useful source of information; this is updated monthly by Coeliac UK and there are a variety of ways to access these updates. Visit www.coeliac.org. uk for more information. Remember that if you have any concerns about your health, contact your GP or healthcare team.

What happens if I eat gluten by mistake?

Getting used to your new diet is a learning process. As with any learning process, there are bound to be mistakes from time to time. If you eat gluten by mistake, don't panic: just try to get back on track with your gluten-free diet straightaway.

The reaction to eating gluten may vary from person to person. In some people, it may trigger immediate symptoms (tummy pain, bloating, diarrhoea, etc) which can last for several days, while in others, no symptoms are seen.

Although it's important not to panic if you accidentally eat gluten, it is very important that you continue to stick to your gluten-free diet.

Eating gluten by mistake will damage the gut, and the effects of this may last longer than any symptoms you may have. Even if you don't have any observable symptoms, the damage is still occurring internally. However, the gut will repair itself once you get back on the gluten-free diet. You may occasionally 'slip up', but this is unlikely to do lasting harm. The important thing is to try to get it right most of the time.

'If you eat gluten by mistake, don't panic: just try to get back on track with your gluten-free diet straightaway.'

Does this mean I can occasionally stray off the diet?

No. If you have been diagnosed with coeliac disease, you need to stick to a gluten-free diet. Any gluten will produce some change to the intestinal lining, whether or not it gives any symptoms. So, even if you aren't aware of it, your intestine is being affected, which can lead to more serious health conditions. So you should try to stick to the gluten-free diet as strictly as possible.

What about oats?

Many people with coeliac disease can eat oats. But sometimes oats are produced in the same place as wheat, barley and rye. This can result in cross contamination if gluten from the wheat, barley or rye becomes mixed with the oats, making the oats unsafe. In addition, a small number of people with coeliac disease may be sensitive even to pure oats (ones which have not been contaminated).

It is up to you to choose whether or not you include pure oats in your diet. Some people prefer not to try them at all, while others do. It is a good idea to speak to your healthcare team, GP or dietitian about this. If you are newly diagnosed, your GP or dietitian may suggest that you avoid oats for around six months to allow your gut to heal. After this, if you decide you want to try oats, you can introduce pure, uncontaminated oats under the supervision of your GP or dietitian. The *Food and Drink Directory* will give you an updated list of pure and uncontaminated oats and oat products, which are also listed in the contacts section at the end of this book.

Coeliac UK advises people with coeliac disease to speak to their local healthcare team, GP or dietitian who can give specific advice on oats and monitor you if you choose to try them.

Labelling

Once you have familiarised yourself with the foods that are naturally gluten free, and those that you need to check, you'll need to get to grips with the system of labelling.

When you are first diagnosed, allow plenty of time for shopping to read the labelling on the products. A law on allergen labelling covers all packaged foods in the UK, and this means that an ingredients list will tell you whether a product contains gluten.

Cereals containing gluten are among the major food allergens that must always be labelled on a pre-packaged product.

So, if a cereal containing gluten is used as an ingredient, it must be listed on the ingredients list, no matter how much or how little is used. Manufacturers must name the grain that has been used, so if you see any of the following words on the ingredients list, you need to be aware that it contains gluten.

- Wheat.
- Rye.
- Barley.
- Oats.
- Spelt.
- Kamut.
- Or any grain which has been made through breeding these together.

At the moment, oats are considered under the law to be a cereal that contains gluten. In future, pure, uncontaminated oats may be labelled as gluten free. See the section on oats earlier in this chapter for more information.

'A law on allergen labelling covers all packaged foods in the UK, and this means that an ingredients list will tell you whether a product contains gluten. Cereals containing gluten are among the major food allergens that must always be labelled on a pre-packaged product.'

Exemptions

Some ingredients which are derived from cereals containing gluten can be processed in such a way that the gluten is removed. These ingredients are safe for people with coeliac disease and so it is not necessary to list the cereal they came from.

The European Commission has worked with the European Food Safety Authority (EFSA) to develop a list of ingredients that are safe for people with coeliac disease. These are:

- Glucose syrups derived from wheat or barley including dextrose.
- Wheat based maltodextrins.
- Distilled ingredients made from cereals that contain gluten (e.g. alcoholic spirits).

Although these originally came from cereals containing gluten, they do not need to be labelled because the gluten has been removed and they are safe. You will sometimes see this listed as, for example, 'wheat dextrose' or 'glucose syrup from wheat' – but they are in fact gluten-free ingredients which are safe for people with coeliac disease to eat.

What is Codex wheat starch?

If wheat flour is washed in water, starch (the carbohydrate part) is dissolved out, leaving the gluten. This is done commercially, creating a specially prepared wheat starch that has had the gluten removed. It is called Codex wheat starch because it complies with the International Codex Standard for gluten-free foods. It is mainly present in the gluten-free foods available on prescription – such as flours and bread mixes. Codex wheat starch can be included in foods that are labelled 'gluten free', but it will be listed as an ingredient.

Codex wheat starch can improve the texture and quality of substitute products, and it is considered safe to eat for most people with coeliac disease. However, a very small number of people may even be sensitive to Codex wheat starch. You should discuss this with your dietitian or healthcare team.

'Codex wheat starch is a specially prepared wheat starch which has had the gluten removed. Codex wheat starch can improve the texture and quality of substitute products, and it is considered safe to eat for most people with coeliac disease.'

Allergy advice boxes

It is recommended that manufacturers use an allergy advice box to warn if there are any allergens present in the product. Remember that allergy advice boxes are not compulsory, so not all manufacturers use them. You can't presume that because there is no allergy advice box the product is safe. Instead, you will need to check the ingredients list.

The Crossed Grain symbol

Coeliac UK has developed its own Crossed Grain symbol.

© Coeliac UK.

When this symbol appears on packaging, it signifies that the food is gluten free. Some supermarkets use their own versions of the crossed grain symbol, but they may not use exactly the same guidelines as those adhered to by Coeliac UK. Make sure that you check the list of ingredients and any allergy advice boxes as well.

The Crossed Grain symbol can make it much quicker and easier to do your shopping. A list of companies which have been approved to use the Crossed Grain symbol are given in the help list.

Other helpful information

Manufacturers use a range of different terms so that people with coeliac disease are able to select food safely. Some of these include:

- Gluten free.
- Suitable for coeliacs.
- Suitable on a gluten-free diet.

'May contain' labelling

The Food Standards Agency (FSA) advises manufacturers on when to label a product with a 'may contain' statement.

Examples of these statements include 'may contain traces of gluten', 'may be made on a line handling wheat' or 'made in a factory where other cereals are present'.

When you see these 'may contain' statements, it means that the manufacturer has decided that there is a risk that the product may be contaminated with gluten. Some manufacturers use the 'may contain' statements even where the risk is very small.

Coeliac UK is able to contact manufacturers to talk through the actual risk of these products. Some products listed in the *Food and Drink Directory* carry a 'may contain' statement, so it's a good idea to contact Coeliac UK for more information on these. Another suggestion is to contact the manufacturer directly for more information about whether the product is suitable for someone with coeliac disease. Customer care helplines or contact details may be listed on the packaging or the manufacturer's website.

'Gluten-free' labelling

In January 2009, new legislation for the labelling of gluten-free foods was published. This is a European regulation (EC 41/2009) and manufacturers have until January 2012 to comply with this legislation.

Recent evidence suggests that most people with coeliac disease can eat unlimited amounts of food with a gluten level of less than 20 parts per million (20ppm). Therefore, food products that contain less than 20ppm can be labelled as gluten free.

This will include foods that are naturally gluten free as well as specialist substitute products, which may contain Codex wheat starch (mainly on prescription), and pure, uncontaminated oats.

The term 'gluten free' implies that it contains no gluten at all. However, in practice there is no 'zero gluten' level. The 20ppm level has been shown through research to be safe for people with coeliac disease, and therefore it is labelled 'gluten free'.

'Very low gluten'

Products that contain between 21ppm and 100ppm can be labelled 'very low gluten'. You will often see this labelling on products that are available in Northern Europe. This will include specialist substitute products, which include Codex wheat starch.

'Suitable for coeliacs'

This means that this product is also safe for people with coeliac disease to eat.

The statements 'gluten free', 'very low gluten' and 'suitable for coeliacs' are all covered by new legislation for the labelling of gluten-free food. When you see these statements, it indicates that the food is suitable for you.

Should I go for products with less than 20ppm (gluten free) or can I have the products that contain 21-100ppm?

People with coeliac disease may have different levels of sensitivity to gluten. Most people with coeliac disease can tolerate a low level of gluten (21-100ppm) without any ill effects. However, some people with coeliac disease are more sensitive and can only eat foods containing less than 20ppm.

It's possible that in the early stages of your diet, when your gut is healing, you may be advised to stick to those foods that contain less than 20ppm to give your body the best chance of recovery. Discuss this with your dietitian or healthcare team.

What about malt extract?

Malt extract and malt flavouring may be made from barley and these can be in a range of foods. Breakfast cereals, ready meals and confectionery often contain barley malt extract. When used in small quantities, the gluten level of the food is likely to be suitable for most people on a gluten-free diet.

However, barley malt extract has to be labelled as containing barley no matter how much is used. Barley will be listed in the ingredients list, as well as in the allergy advice box, if there is one. The *Food and Drink Directory* lists breakfast cereals that contain barley malt extract within the safe level of gluten.

Remember that if you have any concerns about breakfast cereals or any other food products, you can contact Coeliac UK's helpline (see help list).

What about drinks and alcohol?

Coffee, tea and cocoa (but you will need to check drinking chocolate) are all gluten free. Fruit juices are gluten free, but you will need to check fruit squash as a small number contain barley. Cider, wine, spirits, liqueurs, port and sherry are gluten free.

Ales, beers, stouts and lagers are not gluten free as they contain barley. However, some gluten-free beers are available. Whisky and malt whisky are allowed because distilled spirits are gluten free, regardless of the cereal they come from.

Wheat-free/gluten-free products

There are many products available on the market which are labelled as wheat free, and are often stocked in the same 'free from' specialist food areas of the supermarket. Bread which is made from rye flour (which is not gluten free), for example, may be stocked alongside products which are gluten free. Many wheat-free products are also gluten free, but some are not, so you'll need to pay attention, particularly in the early stages.

Keep checking the label

Over time, you will learn to know which products are safe for you to choose. However, it's wise to make sure that you continue to check the ingredients list as from time to time manufacturers may alter their recipe or methods of production.

Summing Up

- Once you have been diagnosed, you should be referred to a dietitian who can advise you on how to make changes to your diet.

- Think of food in three groups: 1. Safe to eat (naturally gluten free) 2. Need to check (may contain gluten) 3. Food to avoid (or replace with gluten-free substitute).

- Specialist gluten-free substitute foods are available on prescription, in most supermarkets, in health food shops and by mail order or Internet.

- If you eat gluten by mistake, don't panic, but do get back onto your gluten-free diet straightaway.

- Some oat products may be contaminated with gluten from other grains; in addition, a small number of people with coeliac disease may be sensitive even to pure oats. Speak to your healthcare team for advice.

- Cereals containing gluten are among the major food allergens that must always be labelled on a pre-packaged product.

- Codex wheat starch is specially prepared wheat starch that has had the gluten removed.

- Allergy advice boxes are not compulsory – check the ingredients list instead.

- Coeliac UK publishes a *Food and Drink Directory* that lists products suitable for a gluten-free diet. This is updated annually, with new updates on individual products given out monthly via Coeliac UK.

Chapter Three

Cooking and Preparing Food

When you're first diagnosed, you may feel concerned about the food you have at home that is not gluten free, particularly if there are others at home that are not following a gluten-free diet. As we saw in chapter 2, as well as making sure that the food you eat is gluten free, you also need to be careful about cross contamination.

Tips for preparing food safely

There are some simple steps you can take to avoid cross contamination:

- Wash down surfaces before preparing food.

- Store gluten-free flours in a separate place from regular flour, in separate tins or boxes if you can.

- Set up a separate toaster (or use toaster bags).

- Use a separate bread board and butter dish (or a different tub of spread) for gluten-free bread to minimise the risk of contamination from breadcrumbs that contain gluten.

- If you are serving different types of food together, serve the gluten-free food on its own plate.

- Use separate cutlery and utensils for butters and spreads and use spoons for jam (or buy products in squeezy bottles if available).

'As well as making sure that the food you eat is gluten free, you also need to be careful about cross contamination.'

- Don't store gluten-free biscuits or cakes in the same tin with non-gluten free cake or biscuits: you may get them muddled up, and you may also end up eating crumbs that contain gluten.

- If you are using a breadmaker, cleaning and hygiene precautions must be taken if the equipment has been used, or is currently used with flours that also contain gluten. You can also check directly with the manufacturer for their advice. Sometimes it's possible to buy additional pans for some breadmaker models so that you can have a separate, gluten-free one.

- Deep-fat fryers which have been used for batter made from regular flour have a risk of contamination.

- Use separate colanders to strain gluten-free pasta and pasta that is not gluten free.

- General advice for food preparation is that you should wash your hands before preparing food: wash hands and nails thoroughly.

Although it may sound daunting at first, you will become used to it and begin to do these things instinctively.

Cooking: the basic rules

Most everyday meals and snacks can be made using gluten-free ingredients. There are also specialist gluten-free cookbooks available with recipes as well as advice on using different combinations of specialist flour. Some recipe suggestions are given at the end of this chapter.

In the early stages of your diet, you may feel quite overwhelmed. It can help to focus on the naturally gluten-free food and plan your meals around them. These foods include:

- Vegetables and fruit (fresh, frozen, dried or tinned).

- Pulses (dried or tinned): these can be added to soups, casseroles and salads.

- Dairy produce (milk, cheese, yoghurts, etc): using low-fat varieties will also cut down on saturated fat.

'Most everyday meals and snacks can be made using gluten-free ingredients. There are also specialist gluten-free cookbooks available with recipes as well as advice on using different combinations of specialist flour.'

- Rice or potatoes (any types).
- Plain meats, fish, eggs.

Any ingredients that contain gluten can usually be exchanged for gluten-free alternatives. Remember to refer to your checklist of the foods you can and can't eat on pages 17-19.

Experiment with gluten-free cooking

When you're first diagnosed with coeliac disease, preparing gluten-free meals can be a challenge. Although it may be frustrating at the start, exploring new and different foods may give you the chance to learn new cooking skills and try out new recipes. If you join Coeliac UK, you'll be given access to the members' area of the website which contains a vast database of recipes to try. *Crossed Grain* magazine also provides some recipes and cooking advice.

Flours

When you're first diagnosed, you may feel the diet is restrictive. However, when you look into the range of different flours available, there's a long list. These include: rice, corn (maize), tapioca (cassava), chickpea (bessan, channa, gram flour), buckwheat, potato, soya and millet.

There are also gluten-free mixes which can be made up of a range of different types of flour.

The baking properties of gluten-free flours can be different from wheat flour. Be prepared for the fact that it may take you a while to find a combination that you are happy with, and try out different recipes.

Xanthan gum

Xanthan gum (pronounced 'zanthun') is a type of starch that is widely used in food and some household goods. It may appear in ingredients lists as xanthan gum or as E415. It is a vegetarian and natural product, and is very useful for baking.

'Xanthan gum is a type of starch that can improve the texture of gluten-free baked products.'

Flours that are naturally gluten free tend to be less elastic in texture than flours that contain gluten. Xanthan gum helps to bind ingredients together and improves the texture of gluten-free baked products when used in recipes as well as in breadmakers. It comes in a powder form and is stocked by some of the major supermarkets in their 'free from' section. It may also be stocked by health food shops as well as by mail order or the Internet. You can also get xanthan gum on prescription.

Will I have to make my own bread?

Many people with coeliac disease (as well as those without!) choose to make their own bread or rolls using a breadmaker or an oven. There are many different types of flour available, and you can experiment with different types. The type of bread you choose to make or buy will depend on your taste and your lifestyle, how much bread or rolls you eat, and whether other people in the household are also following a gluten-free diet.

You'll want to think about bread and flour mixes when it comes to ordering your prescription (see chapter 4). You may want to make sure that you always have some gluten-free sliced bread for toast in your freezer if you have one, and then bake your own fresh bread or bread rolls in smaller quantities. Bread may be one of the main areas that you want to explore when you are first diagnosed, either by trying a number of different types or by experimenting with your own bread or bread rolls.

If you use a breadmaker and toaster, follow the advice given above for preparing food safely. Manufacturers of specialist gluten-free flours may also be able to give advice about using these products in a breadmaker.

If you don't want to make your own bread, there is a huge range of bread and rolls available.

'Bread may be one of the main areas that you want to explore when you are first diagnosed, either by trying a number of different types or by experimenting with your own bread or bread rolls.'

Some basic cooking tips

- Rice noodles are a virtually instant, safe gluten-free food.

- Rice paper wrappers are a great substitute for 'wraps' in place of flour-based tortillas.

- Substitute soy sauce containing wheat flour (and gluten) for gluten-free Japanese tamari soy sauce.

- Rice cakes or gluten-free crackers with hummus or dhal makes a good alternative to sandwiches.

- Buy or make gluten-free pizza bases and create your own toppings.

- Experiment with packed lunches: you may prefer to make open sandwiches or use gluten-free pitta bread, make rice salads or have a baked potato.

Cookery demonstrations

Many local groups hold cookery demonstrations, which can be very helpful, particularly for advice on baking. This may also be a good place to pick up tips from other members.

Crunchy Polenta Fish Cakes

Serves 4

Ingredients
125g brown rice
500g cod or other firm white fish
2 tbsp crème fraîche
1 tbsp fresh coriander, chopped finely
1 tbsp fresh mint, chopped finely
Juice of ½ lemon
3 tbsp polenta
30g gluten-free plain crisps crunched up fairly small
1 tbsp olive oil
Salt and freshly ground black pepper

'A real family favourite, these fish cakes make a great lunch or light supper.'

Method
1. Cook the rice in a pan of boiling water for 30-35 minutes or until very soft. Drain and set to one side.
2. Mash the fish, crème fraîche and rice together, or purée in a food processor, until roughly combined but not smooth.
3. Stir in the coriander, mint, lemon juice and seasoning. Cover and chill.
4. Mix the polenta and crisps.
5. Divide the fish mixture into eight equal-sized portions. Shape each portion into a cake and roll them in the polenta and crisp mixture.
6. Fry the fish cakes in the oil for 5 minutes on each side. Serve piping hot with a leafy green salad.

Cook's tip: replace the polenta and crisps with gluten-free breadcrumbs.

© Kyle Cathie Ltd, *The Gluten-Free Cookbook*, 2006, www.kylecathie.co.uk.

Blueberry Muffins

Makes 12

Ingredients
50g margarine
150g caster sugar
2 eggs
200g rice flour
1 tsp baking powder
175ml sour cream
150g blueberries
½ tsp vanilla essence

Method
1. Preheat oven to 220ºC/425ºF/Gas Mark 7.
2. Cream the margarine and sugar together until light and fluffy. Add the eggs and combine.
3. Sieve the flour and baking powder together and add to the egg mixture with the sour cream.
4. Stir in the blueberries and vanilla essence.
5. Divide the mixture between 12 large muffin cases and bake for 15-20 minutes until golden and risen.

Cook's tip: replace the blueberries with cranberries or sultanas.

© Kyle Cathie Ltd, *The Gluten-Free Cookbook*, 2006, www.kylecathie.co.uk.

'These tasty muffins, bursting with vitamin-packed berries, are great for breakfast or an afternoon treat.'

Gluten-Free Flour Mix

Makes 1kg of flour

Ingredients
300g fine cornmeal (maize) or chestnut flour
500g brown rice flour
200g cornflour

Method
1. Mix all the flours together very thoroughly or put into a food processor and pulse until mixed.
2. Store in an airtight container for up to six months.

© Kyle Cathie Ltd, *Seriously Good Gluten-Free Cooking* by Phil Vickery, 2009, www.kylecathie.com.

Gluten-Free Pizza Base

Ingredients
1 tsp sugar
300ml lukewarm water
2 x 7g sachets dried yeast
300g gluten-free flour (see gluten-free flour mix recipe)
1 tsp xanthan gum
1 tsp gluten-free baking powder
1 tsp salt
1 tbsp olive oil
Topping ingredients of your choice

Method
1. Dissolve the sugar in half the warm water, stir in the yeast, mix well and set aside for 5 minutes for the yeast to start work and froth.
2. Place the remaining dry ingredients in a large mixing bowl, add the yeast mixture and oil and mix well, adding the remaining water a little at a time. Mix through until you have a smooth, fairly wet dough.
3. Cover the bowl with a clean cloth and allow the dough to rise in a warm place for about 15 minutes.
4. Preheat the oven to 200°C/400°F/Gas Mark 6.
5. Divide the dough into two balls. Transfer one dough ball onto a sheet of baking parchment. Cover with a second sheet of parchment on top and flatten the dough out between the papers, to form a 20cm circle. Repeat to make another base.
6. Transfer these bases onto baking trays. Bake the pizza for 8-10 minutes and then remove to add the toppings of your choice.
7. Return the pizzas to the oven, with the toppings and bake for a further 15-20 minutes until bubbling and golden. Serve hot, straightaway.

© Kyle Cathie Ltd, *Seriously Good Gluten-Free Cooking* by Phil Vickery, 2009, www.kylecathie.com.

Birthday Cake Sponge

The glycerine in this recipe helps to keep the sponge softer, as does the butter. Once cooked though it will dry out quickly, due to the rice flour reconstituting itself, so wrap it carefully in foil or eat fresh. Decorate as you wish (using a gluten-free icing).

Ingredients
225g unsalted butter at room temperature
397g tin condensed milk at room temperature
75g potato starch
200g brown rice flour
4 medium eggs, beaten
3 tsp gluten-free baking powder
3 tsp vanilla extract
2 tsp glycerine
3 tbsp olive oil
Butter and brown rice flour, to prepare the cake tins
Filling and decorations of your choice

Method
1. Preheat the oven to 180°C/350°F/Gas Mark 4. Grease two 23cm round cake tins really well, then dust with brown rice flour. Knock out excess flour.
2. Place the softened butter and condensed milk in a mixing bowl and mix them together. Add the starch, rice flour and beaten eggs and stir well.
3. Next, add the baking powder, vanilla extract, glycerine, oil and 3 tbsp of warm water and mix well, preferably with an electric whisk.
4. Spoon or pour the mixture into the prepared tins. Bake for 25-30 minutes, until well risen and lightly browned.
5. Once cooked, leave to cool in the tins. Once cooled, remove from the tins. To finish, sandwich together with your favourite filling and decorate as desired.
6. This cake is best eaten fresh, but you can wrap it in foil or cling film for up to two days until needed.

© Kyle Cathie Ltd, *Seriously Good Gluten-Free Cooking* by Phil Vickery, 2009, www.kylecathie.com.

Brownies

Makes 16

Ingredients
50g best-quality gluten-free dark chocolate
100g butter
200g caster sugar
2 lightly whisked eggs
½ tsp pure vanilla extract
75g ground almonds
½ tsp gluten-free baking powder
Pinch of salt
110g chopped walnuts

Method
1. Line a 20cm square tin with silicone paper.
2. Preheat the oven to 180°C/350°F/Gas Mark 4.
3. Melt the chocolate in a heatproof bowl suspended over a pan of simmering water or in a low oven.
4. Cream the butter and sugar until pale, soft and light, then beat in the lightly whisked eggs, the vanilla extract and melted chocolate.
5. Lastly stir in the ground almonds, gluten-free baking powder, salt and chopped nuts.
6. Spread the mixture in the tin and bake in the oven for about 30-35 minutes.
7. Leave to cool, then cut into 5cm squares for serving.

© Kyle Cathie Ltd, *Healthy Gluten-Free Eating* by Darina Allen and Rosemary Kearney, 2009, www.kylecathie.com.

'Buy a chocolate with at least 70% cocoa solids for real flavour.'

Naan Bread

Makes 6

Ingredients
150ml tepid milk
2 tsp caster sugar
2 tsp dried active yeast
275g rice flour
175g tapioca flour
1 tsp xanthan gum
½ tsp salt
1 tsp gluten-free baking powder
2 tbsp vegetable oil
150ml natural yoghurt, lightly beaten
1 lightly beaten egg

'Add 2 tbsp of chopped spring onions to the dry ingredients for variety.'

Method
1. Pour the tepid milk into a small bowl, add 1 tsp of the sugar and sprinkle in the dried yeast. Sit the bowl in a warm place to allow the yeast to work. After 4 or 5 minutes it should have a creamy, slightly frothy appearance.
2. Sift the rice flour, tapioca flour, xanthan gum, salt and gluten-free baking powder into the bowl of a food mixer. Add the remaining sugar, the oil, yoghurt and lightly beaten egg. Using the paddle attachment, mix the contents together for 8-10 minutes until a smooth and satiny ball of dough is formed.
3. Preheat the oven to its highest setting. Put your heaviest baking tray to heat in the oven and preheat the grill.
4. When the dough is ready, remove it from the food mixer and divide it into six equal sized balls. Keep five of them covered with a clean tea towel while you work with the first.
5. Roll this ball into a tear-shaped naan, about 25cm in length and about 2cm at its widest, using a little rice flour if needed. Roll out a second naan in this way.

6. Remove the hot tray from the oven and slap the two naans onto it. Put it immediately into the oven for 3 minutes. The naan should puff up. Place the tray and naan under a hot grill about 7-10 cm from the heat, for about 30 seconds or until the top of the naan browns slightly. Wrap in a clean tea towel to keep them hot and soft while you cook the rest in the same way.

© Kyle Cathie Ltd, *Healthy Gluten-Free Eating* by Darina Allen and Rosemary Kearney, 2004, www.kylecathie.com.

Summing Up

- As well as making sure the food you eat is gluten free, you will also need to be careful about cross contamination.

- There are some simple steps you can take to prepare gluten-free food safely.

- In the early stages of your diet, it may help to plan your meals around the naturally gluten-free foods.

- The baking properties of gluten-free flours can be different from wheat flour, so you may want to try out different combinations.

- Try out different types of bread and rolls; some manufacturers will give samples.

Chapter Four

Prescriptions

If you are diagnosed with coeliac disease by your GP, you can receive foods such as bread, pasta, flour mixes and other products on prescription. This is one of the many reasons why it's important to obtain a medical diagnosis for the condition. If you have an annual health check, you can also use this opportunity to review your prescription and check that you are getting everything that you are entitled to receive.

What food is available on prescription?

There are many different gluten-free foods available on prescription and new lines are added on a regular basis as manufacturers develop new products.

In the past, people with coeliac disease had a very limited range of prescription foods to choose from, but these days there is a great deal of choice. You can choose from:

- Breads and bread rolls.
- Plain and savoury biscuits.
- Crackers and crispbreads.
- Flour mixes, including speciality cake, bread and pastry mixes.
- Xanthan gum.
- Pasta.
- Pizza bases.

It's a good idea to try out a variety of products before you order them on prescription. Manufacturers will often send you product samples, so ask them to send you details of their full range. You may want to keep a note of the

'If you are diagnosed with coeliac disease by your GP, you can receive foods such as bread, pasta, flour mixes and other products on prescription.'

different types of food you try and your verdict, as even a single manufacturer can produce several different types of bread or rolls. These can vary enormously and you'll want to see and taste what's available.

An up-to-date list of all the foods available on prescription can be found in Coeliac UK's *Food and Drink Directory*.

Who decides what types of food are available on prescription?

The Advisory Committee on Borderline Substances (ACBS), which is an independent body advising the Department of Health, recommend products to GPs (excluding drugs or medical devices) that can be prescribed to patients. An up-to-date list of these foods can be found in the *Food and Drink Directory*. Dietitians may also have a list of these foods. Most GPs will only prescribe products approved by the ACBS, but they are able to prescribe alternatives if they agree that it is needed for your care.

How do I arrange my prescription?

In most parts of the country, the same as for medication, your prescription is created and signed by your GP surgery. You then take the prescription to your pharmacist who dispenses it. When you have worked out the kinds of foods you would like to get on prescription, you can get these on a repeat prescription. However, remember that you may wish to vary your prescription from time to time.

Some Primary Care Trusts (PCTs) run pharmacy-led prescribing schemes which allow you to get gluten-free products from your local pharmacist, rather than via your GP. This is to provide easier access to gluten-free foods and to ease the burden on GPs. Your GP surgery or dietitian can tell you whether this scheme operates in your area. Coeliac UK is currently working closely with pharmacy organisations to assess how these schemes are working. If successful, these schemes may become more widespread in the future.

It's important to speak to your GP if your symptoms change, or if you have any concerns. Your GP can refer you to a dietitian if needed.

Whether your PCT runs a pharmacy-led scheme or not, it's worthwhile building up a good working relationship with your pharmacist. The pharmacist will often have to order food in especially for you and they will have direct contact with wholesalers and suppliers.

How much food can I get on prescription and what sort of food should I choose?

Your dietitian is the best person to advise you on which foods are best for you nutritionally. The amount of food that you can get on prescription is up to your GP.

There are guidelines available that recommend a minimum amount of food that can be prescribed each month. The recommended amount depends on your age, gender, how active you are and whether, for example, you are pregnant or breastfeeding.

The guidelines recommend a minimum amount of units each month. One unit of gluten-free food is equivalent to, for example, a 400g loaf of bread, 200g biscuits or 250g pasta.

'The amount of food that you can get on prescription is up to your GP. There are guidelines available that recommend a minimum amount of food that can be prescribed each month.'

Monthly minimum recommendations

Age and sex	Units per month
Male and female 1-3 years	10
Male and female 4-6 years	11
Male and female 7-10 years	13
Male and female 11-14 years	15
Male and female 15-18 years	18
Male 19-59 years	18
Male 60-74 years	16
Male 75+ years	14
Female 19-74 years	14
Female 75+ years	12
Breastfeeding	Add 4
Last trimester of pregnancy	Add 1
High physical activity level	Add 4

Prescribable gluten-free foods

Food item	Units
400g bread/rolls/baguettes	1
500g bread/flour/cake mix	2
200g sweet/savoury biscuits/crackers/crispbreads	1
250g pasta	1
2 pizza bases	1

Need2Know

The items opposite can be interchanged. For example, in the case of a female aged between 19 and 74, the recommended monthly minimum amount is 14 units. This could be made up of: 8 x 400g loaves of bread or 4 x 500g mixes for bread (8 units), two pizza bases (1 unit), 500g pasta (2 units), 1 x 500g flour mix (2 units) and 200g crackers (1 units).

Remember that how you choose to allocate the units is up to you, in agreement with your GP. The types of food you get on prescription will depend on you and your lifestyle, individual tastes and how you organise your diet and food.

For example, if you decide to make your own bread using a breadmaker, you may choose to receive gluten-free flour or bread mixes on prescription. Alternatively, you may choose to receive ready-made bread or rolls on prescription. Some people choose to use their prescription only for bread, while others may prefer to 'mix and match', getting some bread products in smaller quantities, along with some pasta or crackers. This will depend on your individual tastes as much as anything else. You may decide, for example, that you prefer a brand of crackers sold in shops to ones that are available on prescription, in which case you can use your prescription for other items.

Tip: using the tables, look at which category you fall into, and work out some of the different ways that you could allocate the units.

How do I know how much gluten-free food I will need?

It's a good idea to try to work out how much bread, pasta, etc you would normally eat in a month. A dietitian will be able to help you calculate how much gluten-free food you should be eating. It may take you a few months to work out which foods you would like to get on prescription and to calculate the amounts you're likely to need. It's not advisable to request large quantities of gluten-free food, as some foods do not keep for long periods of time and you'll need space to store it.

Will I have to pay for prescriptions?

Prescriptions for gluten-free food are not free of charge, unless you qualify for free prescriptions. For an up-to-date explanation of who is entitled to free prescriptions, visit the NHS website (www.nhs.uk) and type in 'prescriptions'. All prescriptions are free of charge in Wales.

If you're paying for prescriptions, it's a good idea to look at whether you should get a pre-payment certificate (PPC) as this can work out cheaper if you are getting a lot of prescriptions. This may well be the case if you are getting gluten-free food on a monthly basis. You pay for a PPC in advance, but it covers you for all of your NHS prescription costs, no matter how many you need. There are different types of PPCs available; for details and application forms, please visit the NHS website or ask your pharmacist or GP.

Usually you will need to pay one prescription charge for each line on your prescription, although this can vary between GPs. Eight loaves of the same type of bread would be one charge, while one packet of pasta would be another charge. Check this with your GP when you order your prescription. Remember to check the use-by dates if you order products in bulk, and freeze items if necessary.

'If you're paying for prescriptions, it's a good idea to look at whether you should get a pre-payment certificate (PPC) as this can work out cheaper if you are getting a lot of prescriptions.'

What if I want to change my prescription?

Remember that if you want to change your prescription at any time, you should make an appointment with your GP. Your prescription requirements may change over time depending on your age and level of activity, as well as on other factors such as whether you are pregnant or breastfeeding.

Some people change their prescriptions on a regular basis, while others prefer to keep to the same arrangement once they find out what works for them. It's entirely up to you. However, do remember that new products are regularly added to the list of prescribable foods. As a member of Coeliac UK, you'll receive a new *Food and Drink Directory* each year, and you'll be able to check the up-to-date list of prescribable products. You can also ask your dietitian.

What about other medications?

Other medicines and drugs prescribed to you by your GP will be gluten free. The Medicines and Healthcare Products Regulatory Agency (MHRA) is the government agency which is responsible for ensuring that medicines are safe. MHRA confirms that all of these medicines are safe for people with coeliac disease.

If you take any other medications, be sure to discuss this with your GP when you are first diagnosed. Prescribed medications should only be stopped under medical advice.

Summing Up

- If you are diagnosed with coeliac disease by your GP, you can receive some gluten-free products on prescription.

- There are guidelines available that recommend a minimum amount of food that can be prescribed each month.

- For the purposes of prescriptions, gluten-free food is calculated in units.

- Check to see whether you are entitled to gluten-free food on prescription. If you are not, it may be cheaper to buy a PPC.

- Other medicines and drugs prescribed to you by your GP will be gluten free.

Chapter Five

Eating Out, Travel and Holidays

Can I still eat out?

Many people find that when they are first diagnosed it takes them some time to get to grips with the gluten-free diet at home, as well as the shopping, cooking and food preparation. The thought of eating out can seem very daunting, but in fact, as we'll see, many different types of world cuisine are suitable for people with coeliac disease. It's understandable that you'll feel concerned at the start, but there's a lot that you can do to make things easier.

To recap, you need to make sure that the food you're eating is gluten free. You also need to be careful about cross contamination. This occurs when gluten from other food products comes into contact with gluten-free food and contaminates it. Cross contamination is important because even tiny amounts of gluten may cause symptoms in the short term and damage the gut in the longer term.

Although it can seem that there is a lot to worry about, it's important to bear in mind that people with coeliac disease can (and do) enjoy tasty meals out. People with coeliac disease can (and have) travelled the world, eating gluten free.

'People with coeliac disease can (and do) enjoy tasty meals out, and people with coeliac disease can (and have) travelled the world, eating gluten free.'

Should I call the restaurant in advance?

Yes. Call ahead and see if you can talk to the chef. Make sure that you tell them that you have coeliac disease and that it is a medical condition and not an allergy, or a 'fad diet'. You'll also need to explain to the restaurant why it's vital that they avoid cross contamination in preparing your meal.

When you arrive at the restaurant, talk to the waiting staff and make sure you explain your requirements. Some restaurants routinely offer bread rolls and breadsticks to their customers, or add croutons to soup that may otherwise be gluten free.

Some restaurants and chefs are knowledgeable about coeliac disease, but it can vary. Therefore, it's a good idea to give them specific examples of what is and what isn't safe, for example:

- Breadcrumbs.
- Croutons.
- Wheat flour added to sauces.
- Oil that has been used for foods that contain gluten.

What about the menu?

If you are able to see the menu in advance, this will make the choice easier for you. You can then ask about specific products. If ingredients are bought in, the restaurant should be able to check the ingredients list as these products are covered by the same EU labelling laws as supermarket foods. Look to see if the restaurant offers breaded items, such as fish or chicken in breadcrumbs. If they do, they may be sautéed in the same pan as non-breaded food. You'll need to ask them to make sure that separate pans are used to avoid cross contamination.

Many recipes can be adapted. For example, many salads are gluten free; you will just need to check the dressing and avoid croutons. If the pasta sauces are gluten free, you can discuss taking along your own gluten-free pasta to have with it (make sure that it is strained using a clean colander). You can also ask in advance whether, for example, the restaurant will allow you to take along your own gluten-free bread or roll to accompany a soup or salad that is gluten free. If this is agreed over the phone, make sure that waiting staff are also aware of this on the day.

For desserts, check ice creams, sorbets and meringues. These can be gluten free, but you will need to check. The general advice is 'if in doubt, leave it out'.

If there is nothing suitable on the menu, you can ask if the chef can make something gluten free for you. If they know there is a medical reason for this request, many chefs are happy to do this.

Things to check

If you are having roast potatoes or chips with your meal, it's worth double-checking how they have been cooked. Occasionally, semolina is added to roast potatoes to give them a crispy finish. You'll also need to make sure that the chips have not been cooked in the same oil that is used for gluten-containing products (for example, batter or breadcrumbs). Check too that separate utensils are used so that there is no risk of cross contamination.

You'll need to check soups (in case flour is added to thicken, there is gluten in the stock or croutons are added). You will also need to ask about any dishes with sauces or gravy (don't forget to ask about the stock cubes), as well as coatings on food (for example, check that a steak or a piece of fish has not been dipped in flour before cooking). Remember that sausages may not be gluten free – they may have flour or rusk added as a thickener.

Ask questions

Don't hesitate to question what is in everything, and/or how it is prepared. It is better to be over cautious, as even the smallest amounts of gluten can cause problems. Restaurants that make all their meals from fresh ingredients on the premises will be able to tell you exactly what is in each dish. However, restaurants that use ready-made sauces will need to check with the manufacturer before confirming what is suitable for people with coeliac disease.

'If there is nothing suitable on the menu, you can ask if the chef can make something gluten free for you. If they know there is a medical reason for this request, many chefs are happy to do this.'

Although it can seem very complicated at the start, eating out will become easier as you become more experienced at explaining your condition to restaurants and checking menus. It's also up to you to choose what sort of risks you are prepared to take.

As awareness of coeliac disease increases, restaurants are becoming better at meeting the needs of customers with the condition. Coeliac UK continues to work very hard to raise awareness across the catering industry and this is an ongoing task. There is a dedicated section of their website that contains the latest information for caterers, so it's a good idea to point them in the direction of this.

'Although it can seem very complicated at the start, eating out will become easier as you become more experienced at explaining your condition to restaurants and checking menus.'

Coeliac UK's venue guide

Find out if there are restaurants, cafes or pubs in your area that have been recommended by other Coeliac UK members. Your local group may well have suggestions or see Coeliac UK's venue guide. The most successful restaurant outings I have had with my two children have been based on recommendations from other people with coeliac disease. If you have a good experience, you can share it with other people on the venue guide.

World cuisine

Indian

- Many dishes in authentic Indian restaurants will be suitable. It will be easier to check this if fresh, basic ingredients are used. Many of the dishes made from pulses such as dhals will be suitable, but check that nothing has been added.

- Avoid breads.

- Most dishes are thickened with chickpea flour. This is gluten free but you'll still need to check.

- Poppadums are gluten free. Again, check that no gluten-containing sauces or mixes have been added. Check that they have been cooked in a wok or deep-fat fryer that hasn't been contaminated with gluten from other flours.

Need2Know

Chinese/Thai

- Avoid wheat noodles and soy sauce, and be careful of contamination if dishes that contain gluten are cooked in the same pan as your food.

- Rice noodles and rice-wrapper spring rolls are a good alternative if they are available.

Italian food

- Risottos and dishes made from polenta are good options, as are salads, such as tomato, mozzarella and fresh basil (you will need to check salad dressings).

- Some pizza chains can cook your own gluten-free pizza base if you supply them with one, but you'll need to consider contamination in the kitchen.

Food on the move

It can be harder to obtain a gluten-free 'takeaway' type lunch, particularly in the UK, where the main lunchtime staple is still the sandwich. Larger sandwich shop chains may also stock foods such as rice salads in takeaway tubs (again, check the ingredients) or baked potatoes.

Many people with coeliac disease cope by making sure that they usually carry some snacks with them to have with food such as hummus or cheese, or a bread roll to have with a soup (check that it is gluten free).

'Many people with coeliac disease cope by making sure that they usually carry some snacks with them.'

Other takeaways

There are a few things to bear in mind when ordering takeaways:

- Fish and chip shops: removing batter from fish does not make it safe to eat, as the fish will have already been contaminated with gluten.

- Avoid burgers, sausages and other prepared meats unless they are gluten free.

- Avoid chips if they are cooked in the same oil as battered fish.

Travel

Being diagnosed with coeliac disease should not prevent you from travelling in the UK as well as abroad. You'll need to do some preparation in advance, but you should be able to follow a gluten-free diet anywhere in the world.

Some tips

'Coeliac disease is recognised in a number of different countries. Coeliac UK has information leaflets for over 40 different countries, with language translations that can be used in many other countries.'

- Plan in advance by contacting your tour operator or similar when you book, letting them know that you will require gluten-free meals.

- If you're following a self-catering option, see if you can research the local food and work out what may be readily available. If it's possible, find out what the food labelling is like.

- If you're camping or going somewhere remote, try to find out what's available locally in terms of supermarkets and shops.

- Pack some emergency supplies in your suitcase, depending on where you are going. Supplies such as bread or rolls, pasta, crackers and gluten-free biscuits and cereal bars may be very useful, although you'll need to check about restrictions on flights.

- Toaster bags are very useful to pack, as they will enable you to avoid gluten contamination from toasters that have been used for gluten-containing bread.

Leaflets

Coeliac disease is recognised in a number of different countries. Coeliac UK has information leaflets for over 40 different countries, with language translations that can be used in many other countries. These include contacts for the country's national coeliac organisation, if they have one. Contact Coeliac UK for details.

Travel insurance

Arrange travel insurance and inform the company that you have coeliac disease. Provided you are well and following the diet, costs are usually the same. In EU countries, you'll need to take your EU health insurance card along with travel cover.

Hotels and restaurants

It's advisable to book these in advance and specify that you need a gluten-free diet when you book.

Transport

On airlines, ask for gluten-free meals at the time of booking, and make sure that you remind them when you check in. There's often very little gluten-free food available at airports or ferries or on trains, so make sure you have snacks for your journey, as well as emergency snacks for delays or cancellations.

Taking food abroad

Ask your tour operator whether you can take sealed packets of gluten-free food into the country you are visiting. You may need to obtain a letter from your GP explaining your condition. Some airlines may give you extra baggage allowance if you request it.

Shopping abroad

In Europe and Western countries, gluten-free products are increasingly available. These may be stocked in large supermarkets as well as health food shops and pharmacies.

Although the information in the *Food and Drink Directory* does not apply overseas, remember that all packaged foods in the EU are covered by the same food labelling legislation as in the UK. Manufacturers must list all deliberate ingredients and name the particular grain used. They may also use the word 'gluten'.

Check the travel sheets for each individual country, available from Coeliac UK, before you go.

Remember, when you have coeliac disease, you can still eat out, travel and go on holiday, but it will be easier and more enjoyable if you plan ahead.

Hospital

'When you have coeliac disease, you can still eat out, travel and go on holiday, but it will be easier and more enjoyable if you plan ahead.'

If you have to stay in hospital, whether at home or abroad, make sure that you explain that you need to follow a strict gluten-free diet.

Summing Up

- Plan ahead: if you are eating out, call the restaurant in advance.

- Check the menu in advance if possible and ask questions about the ingredients and how they are prepared.

- Refer the restaurant to the information for caterers on the Coeliac UK website.

- If you are travelling abroad, contact your tour operator or airline in advance to let them know your requirements, and ask Coeliac UK for information leaflets with translations.

- Pack some emergency holiday supplies such as bread, pasta, crackers and gluten-free biscuits.

Chapter Six

Children with Coeliac Disease

How do I explain coeliac disease to my child?

Before they are diagnosed with coeliac disease, children often feel very unwell. Some children may have already worked out that certain foods make them feel poorly.

Once they are on a gluten-free diet, their symptoms will begin to improve. Many parents report seeing a transformation in their child as they make a return to full health and as their energy levels increase.

It's important that you explain the condition to your child in language they understand. There's a fine line to tread. On the one hand, you want them to understand the serious nature of the condition, and the fact that they really mustn't eat gluten. On the other hand, you don't want to frighten your child.

Try to explain in a matter of fact way what coeliac disease is, what gluten does to your child's body and what foods they will have to avoid. Encourage them to ask questions.

Words such as 'disease' can sound quite alarming to a child. You might need to reassure them that it's not 'catching'. They also may struggle to understand words like 'gluten'; you may want to talk about 'foods which make them poorly'. They'll need to know that it's not okay for them to share food with their friends, unless it's safe. Depending on their age, it may be useful to talk them through situations when they may be offered food and to rehearse with them what they might say.

If your child is under the age of seven, Coeliac UK can send you a copy of their special guide for children, called *Me and My Tummy*. This explains the condition through an illustrated story of a child and their family, and is very useful for explaining the condition to younger children. It's also suitable to be used for educational purposes in schools and nurseries.

Some of the specialist gluten-free food manufacturers have their own leaflets or information packs especially for children with information about coeliac disease and recipes. Some may have quizzes or other features. The website www.glutenfree4kids.com is a very useful resource for parents and children.

What can I do to help my child?

'It's a good idea to involve your child in identifying foods that are gluten free to help them understand their diet.'

With relatively small changes to your cooking, it's possible to make many everyday gluten-free dishes that the whole family can enjoy.

It's a good idea to involve your child in identifying foods that are gluten free to help them understand their diet. You can go through the cupboards and mark products that are safe to eat with a smiley face sticker. You could also put a warning sticker on products that aren't safe so that they are able to identify them. You'll need to tell any other carers about the diagnosis too.

Cross contamination

As we've seen in previous chapters, you need to make sure that gluten-free food is prepared without contamination.

If you're catering for a family with different diets, there are some things you can do to make this easier:

- Remember that you will need a separate toaster (or use toaster bags) and bread board. You can label these for your child.

- Have a special gluten-free butter dish or spread and put a sticker on this so your child can recognise it.

- Encourage family members to spoon out jam and marmalade. Consider buying products such as honey and other spreads in squeezy bottles.

You may also find that this is a good time to try to involve your child in cooking, depending on their age. You can take the opportunity to try out new recipes.

How will coeliac disease affect my child?

A diagnosis of coeliac disease may come as a relief for both you and your child, especially if your child has had severe symptoms. Early diagnosis of coeliac disease and treatment with a gluten-free diet minimises the risks of long-term complications associated with the condition. See chapter 10 for more information on associated conditions.

Remember that the gut can take some time to heal, depending on the severity of gut damage at the start. During this time your child may still have tummy aches, but many parents report that within a short space of time their child's health improves greatly.

Some parents find that there can even be unexpected benefits to following a gluten-free diet, as they are more likely to monitor what their child is eating. You may even feel that your child is eating less junk food than they would on an ordinary diet, especially if their diet includes more of the 'naturally gluten-free' food.

There's no denying though that having a lifelong condition that restricts your diet can be difficult for children at times. Encouraging them to talk about it can help. It may also help them to meet other children in the same situation. Local groups may be able to help with this and the Coeliac UK helpline can be a valuable resource.

'A diagnosis of coeliac disease may come as a relief for both you and your child, especially if your child has had severe symptoms.'

Should I have my other children tested?

There is a 1 in 10 chance that if you have a direct relative (parent, brother or sister) with the condition that you will have it too. This means, however, that there is a 9 in 10 chance that your child's sibling won't have the condition. Discuss your concerns with your healthcare team. They may suggest that your child has a blood test for coeliac disease. The NICE guideline on the recognition and assessment of coeliac disease (May 2009) recommends that blood testing be offered to first degree relatives of people with coeliac disease.

Even if your other child/children do not have the condition, you will need to explain the condition to the rest of the family, including siblings, so that they understand what is safe for your child to eat.

My child's already a fussy eater: I'm worried about the additional restrictions

Your dietitian is the best person to advise you about your child's diet. Make a note of any concerns and questions that you have regarding food or nutrition and make sure that you are given a follow-up appointment. You should also mention any concerns you have regarding your child's development to your GP.

As with many aspects of coeliac disease, the early stages of the diet, when you are all getting used to the change, may be the hardest time. Children often have very clear ideas about what they do and don't like, so it will be important for your child to try out different foods before you commit to a prescription. Contact some of the specialist food manufacturers to see if you can get samples.

It may help to involve your child in planning, choosing and cooking gluten-free meals.

Will my child grow normally?

If your child keeps to the diet, they should grow and develop normally. If coeliac disease has gone undiagnosed for a long while, then it may take them some time to catch up. It's important though to make sure that they have their height and weight checked at least on an annual basis, along with any other tests that your healthcare team advises. Your GP or healthcare team will be able to give you more information on this.

As with any medical condition, if you have concerns, go to see your GP.

Follow-up

Make sure that you understand the arrangements for follow-up of your child's care. For example, whether they are expected to attend hospital outpatients department for annual check-ups, or whether this will be done via your GP. Your GP or healthcare team can advise you of this. See also chapter 7.

What about calcium?

Like all children, those with coeliac disease need to have plenty of foods containing calcium to ensure their bones grow healthy and strong. Foods that are rich in calcium include milk (full fat or skimmed), cheese, yoghurt or sardines. Vitamin D is also needed to absorb calcium properly. It is present in some foods, such as oily fish and eggs, and margarines and spreads are usually fortified with vitamin D. Most people get enough vitamin D from exposure of their skin to sunlight.

Your dietitian should discuss your child's intake of calcium, vitamin D and iron with you.

What do I tell my child's school or nursery?

If you join Coeliac UK, they will send you a parents' and carers' information pack which includes a template letter for school, which you can adapt, saving you time. Many schools routinely ask parents to supply information about their child's medical condition, so you should mention coeliac disease on these forms.

The letter you send to your child's school or nursery should include the following:

- That coeliac disease is a medical condition.

- The treatment is a strict gluten-free diet.

- The foods your child is/is not allowed to eat, and whether your child understands this.

- Explain that all those caring for your child will need to be aware of this.

'Make sure that you understand the arrangements for follow-up of your child's care. For example, whether they are expected to attend hospital outpatients department for annual check-ups, or whether this will be done via your GP. Your GP or healthcare team can advise you of this.'

- The arrangements you will be making for lunches.

- You can refer them to www.coeliac.org.uk and suggest the 'food industry professionals' section and the Coeliac UK helpline.

You may also want to include a leaflet or other information, which you can get from Coeliac UK.

If your child goes to an after-school club or any other groups/clubs not run by the school, you will need to inform them as well. Occasionally, children find themselves in situations where snacks or treats are handed out, particularly to celebrate birthdays or for festive celebrations. You may want to make sure that your child's teacher or carer has some substitute treats for these occasions. Remember too that although many fruit cordials or squashes are safe, a small number may contain barley. Check the *Food and Drink Directory*.

'As long as you plan things in advance, there's no reason why your child shouldn't enjoy parties like any other children.'

School lunches

Catering for a child with coeliac disease doesn't have to mean preparing specific gluten-free food. It may be the case that certain changes in practice will mean that the food cooked is safe (for example, cooking chips in separate oil).

The Coeliac UK website has a catering training module that includes a catering toolkit that can be provided for school caterers. Catering guidelines are also available from the Institute of Hospitality – see www.instituteofhospitality.org.

Schools are currently not obliged to provide gluten-free meals for children, so it's a good idea to arrange a meeting with the catering team to see what the arrangements are. Often they can supply you with menus in advance, so you can discuss adjustments to these menus. You can also mention the EU allergen labelling legislation, which will enable them to identify which packaged food is gluten free.

Parties

If you think of your average child's birthday party, foods such as sandwiches, crisps, cake and biscuits tend to feature. These will often contain gluten. However, as long as you plan things in advance, there's no reason why your

Need2Know

child shouldn't enjoy parties like any other children. It's possible to have birthday parties where everyone eats gluten-free food, often without noticing the difference.

Holding your own party

If you're planning your child's own birthday party, there are plenty of things you can do:

- Make gluten-free butterfly cakes, cupcakes or muffins.
- Buy gluten-free cocktail sausages and mini-sausages.
- Have snacks such as cheese and pineapple, grapes and fruit kebabs.
- Make pizza bites using gluten-free pizza or mini pittas.
- Make sandwiches using gluten-free bread or bread and butter fingers.
- Have crudités such as carrot sticks, cucumber and peppers (with gluten-free dips if you think they'll be eaten) or mini rice cakes.
- Check crisp brands and flavours: some are gluten free, some are not (it's advisable only to buy gluten-free crisps as they are often emptied into communal bowls and so may be mixed).

Going to another child's party

When your child attends someone else's party, it can be a little trickier. Although you may want to allow your child to be independent and manage their own diet, it's a good idea to try to discuss your child's dietary needs with the parent holding the party. Again, you'll need to think about issues such as cross contamination without making your child feel uncomfortable. It's often possible to make sure that your child's food is on a separate plate. For the first few parties, you may both feel a little anxious about the situation, but it should become easier as you become more experienced.

Plan ahead

On the day, it's likely that those organising the party will be very busy. Try to have a word with parents in advance of the party and see what types of food they are planning to have. You can then substitute a gluten-free version. Party boxes (available online from party suppliers) can be useful as they can also be used as a plate. Label the box clearly with your child's name, to make sure it doesn't get mixed up with other food.

You can also offer to bring along some gluten-free food for everyone to share. You might want to make some gluten-free cakes or brownies. Alternatively, you could take along a packet of treat-size gluten-free chocolate bars. These can be put into party bags or used as prizes so that your child knows there is a safe treat to eat.

'A useful tip is to try to keep some party treats such as gluten-free mini chocolate bars in your cupboard.'

If the party is taking place at an activity centre, or is part of a special 'birthday package', it's worth ringing beforehand. Often, these parties include a 'meal package' and this may not be gluten free. Check which foods are available and substitute your own gluten-free version. If desserts are branded ice lollies or ice creams, you can check these. You may still want to take along a gluten-free treat for the party bag if there is one.

Sleepovers or trips away from home

Talk to the parent of the child who is having the sleepover or arranging the trip and make sure that they are aware of the basic requirements of the diet and about contamination issues.

For sleepovers, children can take a sealed container or freezer bag of their own gluten-free cereal to which can they add milk. You can also send them with some of their own bread and toaster bags. If you're concerned about contamination in jam or spreads in a non-gluten free household, send along your own. Gluten-free croissants and muffins, which are often individually packaged, make good treats for sleepovers. You'll need to assess the level of risk and work out what is best for your child.

For school trips and days out, give them a packed lunch. Make sure that your child takes some fruit (fresh or dried) or gluten-free crackers, rice cakes or gluten-free fruit or cereal bars as an emergency supply.

Play products

Most play products are gluten free, but some play dough products may contain wheat flour, whether they have been bought in a shop or made at home using 'regular' (i.e. gluten-containing) wheat flour. A recipe is included at the end of this chapter for gluten-free play dough.

Play products will only cause a problem if they are eaten, as you cannot absorb gluten through your skin. But you'll need to take into account that young children may put things in their mouth.

If your child does play with these products, they will need careful supervision to make sure that they do not eat it. Depending on the age of your child, you might prefer to avoid play products containing gluten. Children should be encouraged to wash their hands anyway after playing with arts and craft materials.

If these play products are used at school or nursery, you should mention it to the school.

Cooking/food technology

Children often make small cakes or cookies or have food tasting sessions as part of the primary curriculum. If you plan ahead, there's no reason why your child can't take part. You can provide gluten-free ingredients and remind the teacher about cross contamination.

If your child is studying food technology, you can substitute gluten-free ingredients. This is one of the few areas where food preparation and hygiene, which your child will need to know about, is actually part of the curriculum.

'Most play products are gluten free, but some play dough products may contain wheat flour, whether they have been bought in a shop or made at home using 'regular' (i.e. gluten-containing) wheat flour.'

Coeliac UK and the family

Parents or carers of children under 16 with coeliac disease are welcome to join Coeliac UK on the child's behalf. If there is more than one person with coeliac disease living at the same address, you may want to sign up for household membership.

Membership of Coeliac UK can be especially useful for families. Children go though many different stages – so even when you've got to grips with the gluten-free diet, you'll find that your child faces new challenges at different stages of their development. In the teenage years, due to 'peer pressure' and other pressures, it can be harder to comply with the gluten-free diet, and you and your child may need support with this. Coeliac UK can provide resources to support both parent and child along the way.

'Parents or carers of children under 16 with coeliac disease are welcome to join Coeliac UK on the child's behalf.'

For a parent, 'handing over' the management of a child's gluten-free diet as they make their transition to independence can be difficult. This transition can also be challenging for the young person. More information is given in the following chapter.

Gluten-Free Play Dough

Ingredients
230g rice flour
230g corn flour
230g salt
4 tsp cream of tartar
2 cups water
2 tbsp vegetable oil
Food colouring

Method
1. Place all ingredients in a saucepan.
2. Cook over a low heat for about 5 minutes, stirring all the time. The mixture is very runny to start with but gradually thickens.
3. Remove from the heat and knead on a table or large board to remove any lumps.
4. Roll into a large ball and store in an airtight tub. It will keep for several months.
5. You can also take this along to school or nursery in a labelled ice cream tub.

© Coeliac UK.

Summing Up

- Explain coeliac disease and the gluten-free diet to your child in language they understand.

- Involve your child in identifying 'safe' foods and in choosing, preparing and cooking gluten-free foods (depending on their age).

- Coeliac UK's information pack for parents and carers has useful resources including a template letter for schools and nurseries.

- Early diagnosis of coeliac disease and treatment with a gluten-free diet minimise the risks of long-term complications associated with the condition.

- First-degree relatives of people with coeliac disease should also be tested for the condition.

- Make sure that you are clear about the arrangements for follow-up care for your child.

- If your child has school lunches, meet with the catering team.

- Plan ahead for parties and trips away. If you use products such as play dough, make your own gluten-free recipe.

Chapter Seven

Teenagers and Young Adults

Growing up with coeliac disease can be challenging at times, but there's support available to help you.

Gluten free at home

You'll need to tell the people you live with that you are on a strict gluten-free diet. Explain that although you won't have a life-threatening reaction if you eat gluten, it will damage the lining of your gut and affect your health in the long term. Be prepared to explain to them what gluten is and which foods contain it.

There are some steps you can take to avoid cross contamination:

- Either have your own toaster or use toaster bags for your bread. You can also use kitchen foil on a clean grill.
- Have your own separate butter, spread, pickle and jam pots, and make sure they're labelled.
- Have your own bread board.
- If you're sharing a fridge or food cupboard, be sure to label your food items to remind others not to use them.
- If you use a microwave, you may prefer to have your own containers for heating food in.
- Use cling film, kitchen foil or freezer bags to wrap food in if you are concerned about cross contamination.

When you first move into shared accommodation with others, you may feel embarrassed about having a special diet. However, remember that many people have restricted diets, such as those with nut allergies. Being on a special diet and taking care about how you prepare and store your food may be more common than you think.

If you buy bread or bread rolls in large quantities, or order it on prescription on a monthly basis, it can be useful to have some dedicated freezer space to store it, although this may not be possible in all cases. If you are in a college or halls of residence, see if you can discuss your needs with the student welfare team.

'If you have moved away to a new area, make sure that you register with a new GP as soon as possible. You'll also need to make sure that you have an annual health check or review.'

Out and about

If someone else prepares your food, make sure that they are aware of your requirements. Be aware that you may need to explain the condition if you eat out: you'll need to explain what you can and can't eat. Chapter 5 has more information on eating out and how to approach restaurants to make special arrangements.

Guidelines for caterers can be downloaded from Coeliac UK's website, at www.coeliac.org.uk. You can also contact their helpline for a copy (see help list). You can give this to the catering manager at your work, college or halls of residence to help them understand the condition and how they can adapt their usual procedures for someone with coeliac disease.

Health

If you have moved away to a new area, make sure that you register with a new GP as soon as possible. You'll need to do this so that you can receive gluten-free food on prescription. You may need to discuss your prescription needs with your new GP. You can ask about this when you register.

You'll also need to make sure that you have an annual health check or review.

At your annual review you should:

- See a dietitian, GP or gastroenterologist.
- Have your height and weight checked.

Your healthcare team may want to do some blood tests, such as those for coeliac disease antibodies (EMA and/or tTGA – see chapter 1 for more information).

They may also want to check for nutritional deficiencies by checking your levels of calcium, vitamin D, vitamin B12, folic acid and iron.

Even if you feel well, it's important that you continue to have a check-up on an annual basis. Your dietitian will also be able to inform you of any new products.

Prescriptions

- 16-18 year olds in full-time education are entitled to free NHS prescriptions and dental treatment.
- 16-18 year olds not in full-time education may still be able to get help with prescriptions under the NHS Low Income Scheme, described below.
- 19+ year olds have to pay for prescriptions, even if they are in full-time education. However, they may be able to get help under the NHS Low Income Scheme.

NHS Low Income Scheme

You need to fill out a form to see if you qualify under the Low Income Scheme. The form is available at www.nhs.uk (search 'prescriptions') or by calling 0845 850 0030.

PPC

If you aren't eligible for help under the NHS Low Income Scheme, you might want to think about getting a PPC. If you have to pay for more than five prescription items in four months, or 14 items in 12 months, you could save money in the long run. Many people with coeliac disease do this.

For the PPC, you'll need to fill out a form – also available at www.nhs.uk or by calling 0845 850 0030.

Up-to-date prescription charges can be found on the NHS website or through your GP.

How much food can I get on prescription?

For prescription purposes, gluten-free food is measured in units.

The monthly minimum recommendations for adults with coeliac disease are given below.

Age	Units per month
15-18	18
Male 19-59	18
Female 19-74	14

The figures above are used as a guide to show you the amount of units of gluten-free food you can receive on prescription on a monthly basis.

If you are very physically active, you can add 4 units to the amounts given above.

The units for gluten-free foods are worked out as follows:

Item	Units
400g bread/rolls/baguettes	1
500g bread/flour/cake mix	2
200g sweet/savoury biscuits/crackers/crispbreads	1
250g pasta	1
2 pizza bases	1

Don't forget that how you allocate the units is up to you, in agreement with your GP.

If you're entitled to 14 units, this could be, for example, eight loaves of bread (8 units), plus one packet of rolls (1 unit), one packet of crackers (1 unit), two pizza bases (2 units), two packets of pasta (2 units), equalling 14 units.

What sort of foods should I get on prescription?

How you organise your prescription will depend on factors such as your tastes, lifestyle and cooking facilities. If you make yourself a packed lunch each day, you may prefer to have bread rolls on prescription. Items such as crackers and crispbreads can be useful to have as snacks or for 'emergency supplies'. If you have the space to store them, pizza bases are good to have on hand for easy meals. The *Food and Drink Directory* will give you an up-to-date list of all the products that you can get on prescription.

Remember that if you are ordering your food on a monthly basis, you'll need somewhere safe to store it. Certain types of bread available on prescription may be baked in bulk, or in 'minimum quantities' – so ask your pharmacist when you take in your prescription. There may be a lot to carry and, depending on the use-by dates and storage instructions, you may also need access to freezer space for storage. You can also ask your dietitian for advice at your annual health check.

It may take a little while to get used to organising your prescription and food, particularly if this is your first time away from home, but in time it will become much easier. If you are ever concerned about your diet, or about individual food products, you can call Coeliac UK's helpline (see help list).

Shopping

When you're buying gluten-free food, remember that. by law, cereals containing gluten must be labelled in the ingredients list, even if this is only used in tiny amounts.

Manufacturers also have to say which grain they have used (i.e. wheat, barley, rye or oats).

Don't rely on the allergy advice box (a warning box which tells you if the product contains allergens). Not all manufacturers use these, so you'll have to continue to check the list of ingredients. More detailed information about labelling and ingredients is given in chapter 2.

'Remember that if you are ordering your food on a monthly basis, you'll need somewhere safe to store it. Certain types of bread available on prescription may be baked in bulk, or in 'minimum quantities'. Ask your pharmacist when you take in your prescription.'

Travel

When it comes to travel, there's no reason why coeliac disease should get in your way. You'll need to plan in advance though. Some airlines and tour operators provide gluten-free meals, so ask when you book.

Coeliac UK can provide you with leaflets and translations for most countries. These will have useful phrases that explain coeliac disease and your dietary needs. Visit www.coeliac.org.uk. The website also has details of other coeliac organisations abroad, as well as a Facebook page.

The Coeliac Youth of Europe – www.cyeweb.eu – is another useful site you may want to look at. Much more detailed advice on travel is given in chapter 5.

Alcohol

You'll need to avoid any alcohol containing gluten.

Gluten free	Not gluten free
Gluten-free beer and lager (check the label: specialist gluten-free beer and lager is usually sold in bottles or cans), cider, wine, sherry, port, liqueurs, spirits. Alcopops should be gluten free; however, check the label. If they have used a cereal that contains gluten, it would have to be listed.	Beers, lagers, stouts, ales.

© Coeliac UK.

The recommended 'safe drinking' limits are:

- Men: 3-4 units per day.

- Women: 2-3 units per day.

- A unit equals one small glass of wine, one pub measure of spirits or half a pint of gluten-free beer or cider.

82

It's suggested that you spread the suggested intake across the week, and try to have at least two alcohol-free days over the week. Remember to drink plenty of water too. The Food Standards Agency and the NHS recommend 1.2 litres (6-8 glasses) of fluid per day.

Keeping healthy

▓ Make sure that you continue to receive an annual review/health check.

▓ If you have any concerns about your health, see your GP.

In addition, Coeliac UK has suggested the following 'Top Tips' for a balanced diet:

▓ Eat breakfast – your body needs replenishing with energy every morning, so help kick start your metabolism by having breakfast, such as gluten-free cereal, a fruit smoothie or egg and gluten-free toast.

▓ Eat regularly – this will stop you getting over-hungry and snacking on foods high in fat and sugar, like chocolate, which won't fill you up. Healthy snacks include fresh or dried fruit, gluten-free cereals, yoghurt, rice pudding and custard pots.

▓ Have plenty of iron – iron is important to keep your blood healthy. Some people with coeliac disease do not absorb iron as well as others, resulting in anaemia. Good sources of iron include red meat, poultry, oily fish, dried fruit, baked beans, lentils and peas.

▓ Have plenty of calcium – it is important to include good sources of calcium in your diet to maintain good bone health. These include milk, yoghurt and cheese.

This section has been informed by the leaflet *Moving On: a practical guide for young adults with coeliac disease* that is available at www.coeliac.org.uk.

Summing Up

- Tell the people that you live with that you are on a strict gluten-free diet.

- Take some basic steps to avoid cross contamination in the kitchen.

- If someone else prepares your food, make sure that they are aware of your requirements.

- If you move to a different area, register with a new GP and make sure that you continue to receive an annual health check or review – even if you feel well.

- At your annual review, you should have your height and weight checked and any tests your healthcare team recommends. You may also see a dietitian.

Chapter Eight

Pregnancy, Babies and Weaning

As we've seen throughout this guide, the gluten-free diet is the treatment for coeliac disease. It's important that you stick to the diet. This is the same during pregnancy.

Pregnancy doesn't hold greater risks for women diagnosed with coeliac disease than those without, except in cases where it remains undiagnosed, or if it's not properly managed (i.e. if you are not keeping to the gluten-free diet).

The same general nutritional advice for pregnancy applies to women with coeliac disease as well as women who don't have it, especially with regard to adequate calcium intake and iron intake.

If you have coeliac disease and have any questions – whether you are pregnant or planning a baby – refer to your GP or healthcare team for specialist advice.

Planning a pregnancy

If you're planning a pregnancy (regardless of whether you have coeliac disease or not), you're advised to eat well to assist your chances of conceiving and to give the baby a good start.

'Pregnancy doesn't hold greater risks for women diagnosed with coeliac disease than those without except in cases where it remains undiagnosed, or if it's not properly managed (i.e. if you are not keeping to the gluten-free diet).'

Folic acid

The Department of Health recommends that all women take a folic acid supplement for three months prior to conception, as well as during the first three months of the pregnancy. This helps to prevent neural tube defects. Folic acid supplements are gluten free. It's also a good idea to increase your consumption of folate (the natural form of folic acid) by eating lots of green, leafy vegetables.

Healthy eating during pregnancy

'Remember that your prescription entitlement increases during the last third of your pregnancy and if you are breastfeeding.'

Pregnant women are advised to make sure they get their 'five a day' portion of fruit and vegetables, which are a good source of nutrients and fibre. For starch-based foods that are filling and full of fibre to give you energy, good gluten-free options are jacket potatoes, maize, rice, millet and buckwheat. Try to eat plenty of fresh fruit and make sure that you are drinking enough water. You may also find that dried fruit is good as a snack to keep you going, as it contains plenty of fibre which is important during pregnancy.

General advice on healthy eating during pregnancy is available from www.eatwell.gov.uk.

Alcohol

It's suggested that when you're pregnant it's best to stop drinking altogether. If you do drink, have no more than one or two units, once or twice a week. See www.eatwell.gov.uk or www.drinkaware.co.uk for more information.

Prescriptions

Remember that your prescription entitlement increases during the last third of your pregnancy and if you are breastfeeding (see chapter 4). Think about whether you want to review the foods you are getting on prescription. You may find that you would like to have some gluten-free crackers or crispbreads, which can be useful as snacks. Alternatively, you may want to switch to a type of bread that contains more fibre, or higher quantities of calcium for example. Check the packaging of the product or contact the food manufacturer for more information.

Calcium

Calcium is particularly important during pregnancy; low-fat dairy products are a good source. It's a good idea to discuss whether or not you need calcium supplements during pregnancy or breastfeeding with your GP or healthcare team.

Iron

Remember that iron requirements increase during pregnancy. You'll need to make sure that you have a good intake of iron in your food. Lean meat, oily fish, pulses, eggs as well as dark green, leafy vegetables are all good sources. Dried fruit is also a good source of iron.

Supplements should only be taken on medical advice.

Foods to avoid

The Department of Health recommends that all pregnant women avoid the following, due to increased risk of infection:

- Raw or partially cooked eggs (found in some mayonnaise).
- Mould-ripened unpasteurised cheeses.
- Soft cheeses.
- Patés.
- It is also suggested that women avoid liver during pregnancy as it contains high levels of vitamin A.

If you have any concerns at all about your pregnancy, you should speak to your GP, healthcare team or midwife.

Breastfeeding

According to Coeliac UK, breastfeeding can help protect against coeliac disease in children, and thus delay its onset.

Formula milk

All infant formulas are gluten free.

Weaning babies

If you have coeliac disease, you may be concerned that your baby may have or may develop the condition. There is a 1 in 10 chance of this. However, this also means that there is a 9 in 10 chance that your child won't have the condition.

Even if children have an increased risk of coeliac disease, they should still be weaned in the same way as any other child.

When to wean

General advice is that babies should not be given solids before six months of age. It's accepted that although babies should not in general be given solids before six months, some babies may not be satisfied by milk alone, and so solids are sometimes introduced earlier.

Solids should never be introduced before four months of age.

You can ask your health visitor or dietitian for more advice about weaning.

How to wean

At around six months, babies can begin to eat solid food, along with breast or formula milk. Suitable first foods for babies include pureed fruit and vegetables and baby rice. Your health visitor will be able to advise you on this.

Remember that ready-made baby foods are made according to strict guidelines. Although baby foods may seem bland, you should not add salt or sugar.

You should mention any concerns you have about weaning to your health visitor or dietitian.

When should I introduce gluten into my baby's diet?

At the time of going to press, the current weaning advice given by Coeliac UK is that you should not introduce gluten into your baby's diet until six months of age. There are no benefits in delaying the introduction of gluten after this time. However, some recent research has suggested that the introduction of gluten between four and six months preferably while still breastfeeding could be beneficial. This advice is currently under review, so if you are weaning your child, be sure to check for the latest advice from Coeliac UK, your dietitian or health visitor.

Remember that coeliac disease can only be diagnosed if gluten is in the diet. If symptoms do occur, a diagnosis can be made swiftly and easily.

Signs of coeliac disease in babies

Symptoms of coeliac disease in infants include:

- Diarrhoea.
- Stools often yellow and foul smelling.
- Lower than expected weight gain.
- Generally unhappy.
- Muscle wasting.
- Abdominal swelling.
- Poor appetite.

'Weaning advice, as well as advice on what pregnant women should eat, can change from time to time as new research becomes available. It's important that you check with your GP, midwife or healthcare team for the latest advice, or if you have any other concerns.'

If you notice these symptoms in your baby, you should visit your GP and discuss testing for coeliac disease.

Remember that weaning advice, as well as advice on what pregnant women should eat, can change from time to time as new research becomes available. It's important that you check with your GP, midwife or healthcare team for the latest advice, or if you have any other concerns.

For more advice relating to coeliac disease and pregnancy or weaning, check Coeliac UK's website, which is updated regularly, or call their helpline if you have specific questions. If you are concerned in any way about your baby's health or development, see your GP or health visitor.

Summing Up

- Pregnancy doesn't hold greater risks for women diagnosed with coeliac disease than those without, except in cases where it remains undiagnosed or if it is not properly managed (i.e. if you are not keeping to the gluten-free diet).

- The same general nutritional advice for pregnancy applies to women with coeliac disease as well as women who don't have it, especially with regard to adequate calcium intake and iron intake.

- The Department of Health recommends that all women take a folic acid supplement for three months prior to conception, as well as during the first three months of the pregnancy.

- General advice on healthy eating during pregnancy is available from www.eatwell.gov.uk.

- Your prescription entitlement increases during the last third of pregnancy and if you are breastfeeding.

- If you have any concerns at all about your pregnancy, you should speak to your GP, healthcare team or midwife.

- Even if children have an increased risk of coeliac disease, they should still be weaned in the same way as any other child. Coeliac disease can only be diagnosed if gluten is in the diet.

- Weaning advice as well as advice on what pregnant women should eat can change from time to time. It's important to check with your GP, midwife or healthcare team for the latest advice, or if you have any other concerns.

Chapter Nine

Staying Healthy: Support and Follow-Up

Support and follow-up

Once you're diagnosed, your most important task is to keep to a gluten-free diet. If you keep to a strict gluten-free diet you are giving yourself the best possible chance of staying healthy, as well as reducing the risk of certain related health conditions such as osteoporosis (see chapter 10).

Once you're established on the diet, you should begin to feel much better. However, even if you feel well you should still attend follow-up appointments on a regular basis.

What to expect from your healthcare team

After the initial diagnosis, it's recommended that you see a registered dietitian after three months, six months and 12 months. If well, you should then be reviewed on an annual basis, or sooner if problems arise.

Dietitians can keep you up to date with new advances and products. Many people, when they are first diagnosed, may be deficient in some key nutrients. The dietitian can support you in making sure that you're eating a balanced diet.

After this, you should be followed up annually. Guidelines produced by the British Society of Gastroenterology suggest that an annual check-up be carried out by your GP, outpatient gastroenterology clinic or dietitian.

'After the initial diagnosis, it's recommended that you see a registered dietitian after three months, six months and 12 months. If well, you should then be reviewed on an annual basis or sooner if problems arise.'

The arrangements for follow-up may vary, depending on where you live and which PCT is responsible for you. Make sure that you know who is responsible for your annual check-up.

What happens at my annual check-up?

The purpose of the check-up is to make sure that your coeliac disease is under control and that you are sticking to your gluten-free diet.

The appointment may include some routine blood tests such as:

- Coeliac disease antibodies (EMA and tTGA).

- Haemoglobin, red cell folate, serum ferritin, serum albumin and alkaline phosphatase.

- Tests for possible nutritional deficiencies, particularly if these were present before diagnosis – for example, calcium, vitamin D and vitamin B12.

What about a DEXA scan?

Depending on how old you were when you were diagnosed, you may also be referred for a bone scan or DEXA (Dual Energy X-ray Absorptiometry) scan to check whether there is any evidence of low bone density (osteopenia) or osteoporosis. Both of these conditions are discussed in more detail in chapter 10.

Healthy gluten-free living

Balanced eating

Once you are on a gluten-free diet, your gut lining should heal and the absorption of nutrients should return to normal. You may put on weight more easily as a result of this.

Eating a balanced diet and keeping a healthy weight reduces the risk of a number of diseases associated with obesity and being overweight, including heart disease and Type 2 diabetes. Healthy eating recommendations for weight control and a healthy heart are the same for all people, whether they have coeliac disease or not.

However, what is very important for people with coeliac disease is making sure that they eat plenty of calcium in their diet to keep their bones healthy and to reduce the risk of osteoporosis.

Your dietitian can assess your diet and give you advice to meet your individual needs.

There is no reason why people with coeliac disease cannot eat healthily. Naturally gluten-free foods which are safe for you include fruit, vegetables, dairy products, pulses and rice. These are all foods that form part of a healthy diet whether a person has coeliac disease or not.

Remember that even if you are on a gluten-free diet, you should still be trying to eat a balanced diet.

Seven steps to a balanced gluten-free diet

Coeliac UK recommends seven simple steps that you can take towards making sure that you have a balanced, gluten-free diet:

1. Eat regular meals based on starchy carbohydrate foods such as:

- Rice (all types: basmati, wild, aromatic, brown, white, long grain, Arborio).

- Potatoes (all types).

- Yams, plantains.

- Gluten-free grains such as polenta (cornmeal), buckwheat, millet, quinoa, teff and sorghum.

- Gluten-free breads and pastas.

These foods are a good source of energy and can also provide fibre, calcium, iron and vitamin B. Gluten-free grains are available from larger supermarkets or health food shops.

'Eating a balanced diet and keeping a healthy weight reduces the risk of a number of diseases associated with obesity and being overweight, including heart disease and Type 2 diabetes.'

Avoid adding too much fat, such as oil, butter or margarine, to these foods – the extra calories can lead to weight gain.

2. Aim to eat five portions of fruit and vegetables a day.

Fruit and vegetables are naturally gluten free, high in fibre, low in fat and help to fill you up. They're also rich in antioxidant vitamins and minerals, which provide a range of health benefits relating to chronic diseases, including preventing heart disease and some cancers.

Try to include different types in your diet and make the most of seasonal fruit and vegetables.

A portion of fruit or vegetable can be:

- One medium fruit, for example an apple.

- Two small fruits, such as plums.

- A small handful of very small fruit, for example grapes.

- A bowlful of salad.

- Three tbsp of any type of vegetable (fresh, frozen, dried or tinned all count).

To maximise your fruit and vegetable intake, try to add salad or use vegetables to 'bulk up' meals. You can also use more pulses, such as peas, beans or lentils in stews and soups, as well as adding extra vegetables on gluten-free pizza.

3. Reduce total fat intake, especially saturated fat.

There are three basic types of dietary fat. All of them contain the same amount of energy (calories) per gram, but all of them have different effects on the body.

Saturated fats are found in animal products, including lard, butter, fatty cuts of meat and full-fat dairy products. Hidden sources include processed foods, such as gluten-free pastries, biscuits and cakes. These fats can raise cholesterol levels, and therefore increase the risk of heart disease.

To reduce your saturated fat intake:

- Choose lean cuts of meat and remove any skin from poultry before cooking.

- Steam, poach, boil, grill, bake or microwave foods instead of frying.

'Fruit and vegetables are naturally gluten free, high in fibre, low in fat and help to fill you up. They're also rich in antioxidant vitamins and minerals, which provide a range of health benefits.'

Need2Know

- Choose low-fat dairy products that contain as much calcium as full-fat options.

Polyunsaturated (sunflower/corn oil) and monounsaturated (olive/rapeseed oil) fats come from vegetable sources. Where possible, use these as substitutes for saturated fats, but be careful to use only a small amount. If you use oil in cooking, you may find it useful to measure it out using a tsp or tbsp. One tbsp of oil contains around 125 calories.

Omega 3 is a type of polyunsaturated fat that can help to thin the blood and can also have anti-inflammatory properties. Good sources of omega 3 oils are oily fish (fresh, frozen and tinned) such as mackerel, sardines, pilchards, salmon, trout, herring, kippers and fresh (not tinned) tuna.

It is generally recommended to aim for two portions of fish per week, one of which should be oily. If you have a history of heart disease and/or angina, or if you are pregnant or breastfeeding, you should discuss your oily fish intake with your GP or dietitian.

Alternative plant sources of omega 3 fats include walnuts, rapeseed, flaxseed, linseed, corn and sunflower oils.

4. Cut down on sugar and sugary foods.

A diet high in sugar can contribute to weight gain and tooth decay. Sugar is often added to foods such as sweets, biscuits, cakes and full-sugar fizzy drinks.

Try to:

- Limit the amount of these foods.
- Choose diet or reduced sugar fizzy drinks.
- Choose tinned fruit in natural juice instead of syrup.
- Add water to dilute fruit juices.

5. Eat plenty of fibre.

A high fibre diet promotes healthy bowel function and can help to control cholesterol levels. It can also help you to feel full, which may in turn help you to maintain a healthy body weight.

Good sources of fibre include:

- Brown rice.

- High fibre/multigrain gluten-free breads.

- Pulses (beans, peas, lentils).

- Nuts and seeds, fruit and vegetables (especially those with skins, pips and seeds).

- Potatoes in their skins.

6. Cut down on salt.

Too much salt (sodium) is linked to high blood pressure, heart disease and strokes. Most of the salt we consume is already in bought foods such as soups, cheese, gluten-free breads and cereals. Foods that are particularly high in salt include processed foods, ready meals and snacks such as crisps and nuts.

Try to:

- Aim to eat less than 6g per day (i.e. one tsp of salt, or 2.5g of sodium).

- Limit high-salt foods.

- Try not to add salt when cooking or at the table.

- As a healthier alternative, use herbs and spices for flavouring food.

7. Drink alcohol within sensible limits.

The recommended maximum intake of alcohol for women is 2-3 units a day, while for men it's 3-4 units per day. A unit equals half a pint of cider or gluten-free beer, one small glass of wine, or one pub measure of spirits.

Plan at least two alcohol-free days per week and spread your allowance out across the week, rather than 'binge drinking'.

Making balanced choices

When you are diagnosed with coeliac disease, you may spend a lot of time reading the labels to check for information regarding gluten.

You may also notice other types of food labelling to help people select food products for balanced eating.

'Traffic light' labelling

The Food Standards Agency (FSA) has approved what is called a traffic light system, designed to help you select healthier foods more easily.

- Red = high.
- Amber = medium.
- Green = low.

The idea is that you should choose more greens and ambers (and fewer reds) when selecting food, if you want to make a healthier choice.

GDA labelling

Some manufacturers use the GDA (guideline daily amount) scheme, developed by the Institute of Grocery Distribution. It gives you a guide to the energy and nutrients an individual needs for a balanced diet. For more information, see www.igd.com.

Exercise

If your coeliac disease has been undiagnosed for a while, a lack of energy may be one of your symptoms. However, once you are established on the diet and you are feeling better, you will be able to do exercise.

If you have coeliac disease, it's especially important that you try to include some weight-bearing exercise in your routine, as weight-bearing exercise is needed for good bone health. Weight-bearing activity is any activity where you support the weight of your own body, for example brisk walking, jogging, dancing, skipping or aerobics. It doesn't need to be excessive, but it's good if you aim to do at least 30 minutes each day of an activity such as brisk walking.

It's important that you check with your GP before you start a new activity or exercise programme, especially if you have been inactive for a long period of time.

'If you have coeliac disease, it's especially important that you try to include some weight-bearing exercise in your routine, as weight-bearing exercise is needed for good bone health.'

Summing Up

- Keep to a gluten-free diet: you are giving yourself the best possible chance of staying healthy.

- After the initial diagnosis, it's recommended that you see a registered dietitian after three months, six months and 12 months. If well, you should then be reviewed on an annual basis, or sooner if problems arise.

- Even if you are on a gluten-free diet, you should still be trying to eat a balanced diet. Follow Coeliac UK's seven steps to a balanced gluten-free diet.

- It's important to include some weight-bearing exercise in your routine as it is needed for good bone health.

- Check with your GP before you start a new activity or exercise programme, especially if you have been inactive for a long period of time.

Chapter Ten

Coeliac Disease and Associated Conditions

Coeliac disease is a lifelong condition and the treatment is a gluten-free diet. Keep to the gluten-free diet and look after yourself by having regular health checks (guidelines suggest follow-up at three, six and 12 months after diagnosis). If well, you should then be reviewed on an annual basis (or sooner if problems arise). Regular follow-up checks by your healthcare team, who are experienced in the management of coeliac disease, mean that any symptoms you may develop can be monitored. You can also receive specialist advice.

Undiagnosed coeliac disease has health implications. Evidence reviewed for the NICE guideline published in May 2009 highlighted an increased risk of Hodgkins and non-Hodgkins lymphoma, as well as cancer of the small bowel. The NICE guideline also states that there is no overall increased risk for all cancers in people with coeliac disease. Equally, undiagnosed coeliac disease can lead to unexplained infertility and an increased incidence of miscarriage. However, remember that this is when coeliac disease is undiagnosed.

Some other health conditions associated with coeliac disease are described overleaf. Remember, these conditions are associated with coeliac disease. It doesn't necessarily mean that you will have them, or develop them.

If you have any concerns about your health, make sure you see your GP or healthcare team.

'Regular follow-up checks by your healthcare team, who are experienced in the management of coeliac disease, mean that any symptoms you may develop can be monitored. You can also receive specialist advice.'

Dermatitis herpetiformis

Dermatitis herpetiformis, often referred to as 'DH', is a skin condition that's linked to coeliac disease. DH affects fewer people than coeliac disease (it's thought to affect around 1 in 10,000 people). Although it can appear at any age, it's most commonly diagnosed in people between the ages of 15 and 40, and is rare in children. Typical symptoms are red raised patches (often with blisters that burst with scratching), severe itching and stinging. The rash is usually on the elbows, knees and buttocks, but any area of the skin can be affected. It's diagnosed by a simple test called a skin biopsy. Anyone with a positive skin biopsy result should then be referred to a gastroenterologist for a gut biopsy, the same test used in diagnosing coeliac disease. Even though most people with DH do not complain of gut symptoms (such as stomach pain and bloating), most people with DH have the same kind of gut damage that is seen with coeliac disease.

The treatment for DH, like coeliac disease, is a gluten-free diet. Anyone who is medically diagnosed with DH can join Coeliac UK as a member.

Lactose intolerance

'When the gut is inflamed (as it is in newly diagnosed or untreated coeliac disease), there can be a deficiency in lactase. This is because lactase is found in the villi, which are flattened and reduced in undiagnosed coeliac disease.'

Lactose is the type of sugar present in milk, which is digested by the enzyme lactase that is present in the small intestine. If this enzyme is deficient, the symptoms of lactose intolerance can occur. These include nausea, bloating and abdominal discomfort; symptoms which are very similar to those of coeliac disease.

In a small number of people, this is a permanent genetic problem and they have to avoid products containing lactose.

However, when the gut is inflamed (as it is in newly diagnosed or untreated coeliac disease), there can be a deficiency in lactase. This is because lactase is found in the villi, which are flattened and reduced in undiagnosed coeliac disease (see chapter 1).

If you believe you may be lactose intolerant, do not immediately cut lactose from your diet. The first step would be to discuss your concerns with your dietitian. People with lactose intolerance can usually tolerate small amounts of lactose in their diet such as milk in drinks and possibly cheese or yoghurt, but you may need to limit the amount of dairy products containing lactose you have. This is while the gut is still inflamed. Once the gluten-free diet is established and the gut is less inflamed, most people are able to tolerate milk products again. In this case, lactose intolerance is a secondary, temporary problem, linked to the gut inflammation.

It is important for all people to make sure they have plenty of calcium in their diet. When you have coeliac disease, this is especially important. Whether you are restricting your lactose intake or not, you must make sure that foods containing a rich source of calcium are included in the diet. A dietitian is the best person to advise you about your diet.

Osteoporosis

People with coeliac disease are at greater risk of low bone density (osteopenia) and osteoporosis (the later stage of the condition). This is thought to be due to decreased absorption of calcium. The National Osteoporosis Society reports that one study showed that half of those with coeliac disease had low bone density, especially if they were diagnosed later in life, were underweight or were post-menopausal women. The risks for osteoporosis are greater if your coeliac disease has gone undetected for a longer period of time.

To put this into context, you need to remember that all bones naturally become less dense with age. The percentages of people with both osteopenia and osteoporosis increase substantially as people get older.

Depending on your age at diagnosis, you may be referred for a bone scan or DEXA scan which will assess your bone density. This is something you should discuss with your healthcare team. Coeliac UK can also provide more information on osteoporosis, as well as the National Osteoporosis Society (see help list).

As well as keeping to the gluten-free diet, make sure that you have adequate calcium and vitamin D (which is needed in order to absorb calcium properly). General advice for producing healthy bones includes regular, weight-bearing exercise, stopping smoking and keeping within acceptable drinking limits.

'If you believe you may be lactose intolerant, do not immediately cut lactose from your diet. The first step would be to discuss your concerns with your dietitian.'

It's important that you discuss any concerns that you may have about osteoporosis with your GP or healthcare team.

Other autoimmune diseases

Coeliac disease belongs to a group of conditions known as autoimmune diseases. An autoimmune disease is a reaction to a trigger, which causes the body to attack itself. In coeliac disease, the trigger is gluten. There is a group of autoimmune diseases which occur in people who probably have an inherited predisposition to develop them, probably because they have a genetically more 'sensitive' immune system. For this reason, coeliac disease is more common among people with other autoimmune diseases, such as Type 1 diabetes and autoimmune thyroid disease.

Coeliac disease and Type 1 diabetes

'There is a link between coeliac disease and Type 1 diabetes. Managing the diet for both these diseases together requires professional guidance from a registered dietitian.'

There is a link between coeliac disease and Type 1 diabetes. This is probably because they both have a common genetic predisposition – HLA-DQB1 is the gene present in the majority of people with both conditions. There is no increased risk of coeliac disease in people with Type 2 diabetes. NICE guidelines state that 2-10% of people with coeliac disease will also have Type 1 diabetes. In most cases (about 90%), Type 1 diabetes is diagnosed before coeliac disease. The NICE guidelines recommend that anyone with Type 1 diabetes should be screened for coeliac disease. Managing the diet for both these diseases together requires professional guidance from a registered dietitian.

When you have coeliac disease as well as Type 1 diabetes, it is essential that you receive specific dietary advice and ongoing support from your local healthcare team. Contact information for Diabetes UK is given in the help list.

Coeliac disease and thyroid disease

The link between coeliac disease and autoimmune thyroid disease is well established. The NICE guidelines on the recognition and diagnosis of coeliac disease say the prevalence of autoimmune thyroid disease in people with coeliac disease is up to 7%. Another study in 2005 found that in a group of patients with coeliac disease, 26.2% had autoimmune thyroid disease, compared to 10% of control subjects.

Summing Up

- People with coeliac disease are at greater risk of low bone density (osteopenia) and osteoporosis (the later stage of the condition). This is thought to be due to decreased absorption of calcium.

- As well as keeping to the gluten-free diet, make sure that you have adequate calcium and vitamin D (which is needed in order to absorb calcium properly).

- It's important that you discuss any concerns that you may have about osteoporosis or any other health conditions with your GP or healthcare team.

- There is a link between coeliac disease and other autoimmune diseases, such as Type 1 diabetes and thryroid disease.

- Keep to your gluten-free diet and continue to receive annual healthchecks, even if you feel well.

Chapter Eleven

Frequently Asked Questions

How common is coeliac disease?

Research has shown that coeliac disease affects 1 in 100 people in the UK, making it much more common than previously thought. However, many people are undiagnosed; it's thought that around 500,000 people have not yet been diagnosed.

How is coeliac disease different from other food allergy?

For a start, coeliac disease is not a food allergy or food intolerance. It's an autoimmune disease and the trigger is gluten. Gluten causes an abnormality in the gut. In the long term, this damage can lead to other health problems. Although the abnormality is caused by the immune system's response, this type of immune response is very different to an 'allergic reaction' (in the sense of a nut allergy, for example). In most cases of food allergy, there is no abnormality caused to the intestine.

Although food allergies and intolerances do exist, they should not be confused with coeliac disease.

Can children grow out of it?

If coeliac disease is correctly diagnosed, it is a lifelong condition. Although individual levels of sensitivity to gluten may vary, and some children may seem to have no symptoms if they eat it, you have to remember that eating gluten will still be causing damage to the intestine. That's why it's important to keep to a gluten-free diet for life, even if you have no apparent symptoms when you eat gluten. Children and teenagers with coeliac disease on a gluten-free diet are healthy, grow normally and can do the same things as other children.

If I keep on the diet until my gut has healed, is it OK to have the occasional treat containing gluten?

Coeliac disease is a lifelong condition. If you keep to the diet and avoid gluten, then you should enjoy normal health. If you eat gluten, even from time to time, it will be causing damage internally to the gut, even if you don't feel any symptoms. If you have coeliac disease and continue to eat gluten, you are increasing your risk of other health complications. So, it's best to keep to a strict gluten-free diet.

I have coeliac disease and I'm planning a baby: am I at greater risk?

If keeping to a gluten-free diet and in good health, pregnant women with coeliac disease are not thought to be at any greater risk than other women. Adverse health outcomes in pregnancy (such as miscarriage) have been linked in research to untreated coeliac disease. See chapter 8 for more advice.

Do I need to check whether cosmetics contain gluten, and will they cause me problems?

For gluten to cause problems, it needs to be eaten, so just touching it or putting it on the skin should not in theory cause problems. However, children are advised to avoid products such as play dough (made from wheat flour), so you could replace suspect products with a product that is gluten free in case they accidentally eat the product.

I've been diagnosed with coeliac disease: can I still drink beer?

Regular beers, ales, stouts and lagers contain gluten (barley) and need to be avoided. However, there are now some gluten-free beers available. Check the help list for contact details.

Should I avoid exercise?

When you are first diagnosed, you may still be feeling unwell (tiredness, lethargy), particularly if you have had symptoms for a long time. It's possible you may be deficient in some nutrients or anaemic (low in iron), making you feel tired. However, once your diet is established, you should begin to feel a lot better. After that, it's good to exercise for your general health. Exercise is important in reducing your risk of osteoporosis. Remember to check with your GP before starting a new activity, particularly if you have been inactive for a long time.

I have coeliac disease: will I still be able to obtain insurance?

There should be no difficulty obtaining life or travel insurance. Insurance companies will ask for a medical report from your GP. The premium may be slightly increased in the early years after diagnosis, but after you have enjoyed good health for some time, your insurance should be similar to people without coeliac disease. Make sure that you obtain proper advice from an insurance adviser or independent financial adviser, and shop around for different quotations if you are unhappy.

I've just been diagnosed with coeliac disease and I am a vegetarian: will I need to take dietary supplements?

It's possible to eat a gluten-free diet if you are vegetarian. Like all people with coeliac disease, you need to try to eat a balanced diet with adequate intake of essential nutrients. A dietitian will be able to give you specific advice on this, which may also include advice about dietary supplements. Ask your dietitian or healthcare team about this.

I've seen a lot of wheat-free products in supermarkets: can I eat these?

Many specialist wheat-free products are also gluten free and you can eat these. However, remember that some 'wheat-free' products are not gluten free. Products made from barley or rye, which both contain gluten, are wheat free but not gluten free. These are not safe for you to eat. Remember to read the ingredients list. For advice on Codex wheat starch, see chapter 2.

I have coeliac disease and I'm on a gluten-free diet. Does it matter what I eat, as long as it's gluten free?

If you have coeliac disease, it's easy to become so preoccupied about avoiding gluten that you may overlook other basic principles of healthy eating. You need to eat a gluten free diet, but also a balanced diet that will help to ensure an adequate intake of essential nutrients (such as calcium and iron). Your annual health check is an important source of advice for this. See chapter 9 for advice on staying healthy.

Is there a cure for coeliac disease?

As with many other health conditions, research is being carried out all the time on the condition. However, at the moment the only known treatment is a gluten-free diet.

I have coeliac disease: do I need to have a bone scan?

Depending on their age at diagnosis, some people with coeliac disease are offered a bone scan (also known as a DEXA scan) when they are first diagnosed. Others may be offered scans later on – this depends from person to person. If you continue to receive your annual health check, this is the kind of issue that will be discussed with you. See chapter 10 for more information.

Help List

Health

British Dietetic Association (BDA)

5th floor, Charles House, 148/9 Great Charles Street, Queensway, Birmingham, B3 3HT
Tel: 0121 200 8080
www.bda.uk.com
The BDA is a professional association for dietitians.

British Society of Gastroenterology (BSG)

3 St. Andrews Place, Regent's Park, London, NW1 4LB
Tel: 020 7935 3150
www.bsg.org.uk
The BSG helps to promote high standards of patient care in gastroenterology. Their website has clinical information on digestive disorders and research.

Coeliac UK

3rd Floor, Apollo Centre, Desborough Road, High Wycombe, HP11 2QW
Tel: 0845 305 2060 (helpline)
www.coeliac.org.uk
Coeliac UK is a registered charity and the national organisation for people with coeliac disease and dermatitis herpetiformis. It publishes the annual *Food and Drink Directory* and has a helpline, an extensive website and many resources. Coeliac UK can also put you in touch with a local support group in your area. Different types of membership are available.

Coeliac Youth of Europe

www.cyeweb.eu
Information on travelling and coeliac disease. The main aim of the organisation is to raise awareness and exchange knowledge.

Diabetes UK (England)

Macleod House, 10 Parkway, London, NW1 7AA
Tel: 020 7424 1000
info@diabetes.org.uk
www.diabetes.org.uk

Diabetes UK (Northern Ireland)

Bridgewood House, Newforge Business Park, Newforge Lane, Belfast, BT9 5NW
Tel: 028 9066 6646
n.ireland@diabetes.org.uk

Diabetes UK (Scotland)

The Venlaw, 349 Bath Street, Glasgow, G2 4AA.
Tel: 0141 245 6380
scotland@diabetes.org.uk

Diabetes UK (Wales)

Argyle House, Castlebridge, Cowbridge Road East, Cardiff, CF11 9AB
Tel: 029 2066 8276
wales@diabetes.org.uk

Diabetes UK is the largest organisation in the UK working for people with diabetes, funding research, campaigning and helping people live with the condition.

Gluten Free For Kids

www.glutenfree4kids.com
Website aimed at parents of children with coeliac disease.

National Institute for Health and Clinical Excellence (NICE)

MidCity Place, 71 High Holborn, London, WC1V 6NA
Tel: 0845 003 7780
nice@nice.org.uk
www.nice.org.uk

NICE is an independent organisation responsible for providing national guidance on promoting good health and preventing and treating ill health.

NHS Choices (England)

www.nhs.uk
Northern Ireland
www.hscni.net
Scotland
www.nhs24.com
Wales
www.wales.nhs.uk
NHS Choices is a comprehensive information service that helps to put you in control of your healthcare.

The National Osteoporosis Society

Camerton, Bath, BA2 0PJ
Tel: 0845 450 0230 (helpline)
info@nos.org.uk
www.nos.org.uk
The National Osteoporosis Society is the only UK-wide charity dedicated to improving the diagnosis, prevention and treatment of osteoporosis.

Diet

Advisory Committee on Borderline Substances

ACBS@pasa.nhs.uk
www.pasa.nhs.uk/PASAWeb/Productsandservices/Pharmaceuticals/ACBS.htm
The Advisory Committee on Borderline Substances (ACBS) is the committee responsible for advising approved prescribers on the prescribing of certain foodstuffs and toiletries.

Drink Aware

www.drinkaware.co.uk
Organisation aiming to change the public's drinking habits and promote responsible drinking.

Eatwell

www.eatwell.gov.uk
Packed with reliable and practical advice about healthy eating.

European Food Safety Authority (EFSA)

www.efsa.europa.eu
The EFSA is an independent source of scientific advice and communication on risks associated with the food chain.

Food Standards Agency (FSA)

www.food.gov.uk
An independent government department set up to protect the public's health and consumer interests in relation to food.

Institute of Grocery Distribution

www.igd.com
The Institute of Grocery Distribution is a team of experts dedicated to the development of the food and grocery industry and committed to the needs of its consumers. It is a registered charity.

Gluten-free food companies

Many of the products from the stockists listed below are available on prescription. Check the websites as new product and prescription ranges are added regularly. Contact manufacturers direct for samples.

Dietary specials

www.dietaryspecials.co.uk
A large range of products that are gluten free as well as wheat free, recipes and other features. Products and stockist information can be found on the website.

Genius Gluten Free

www.geniusglutenfree.com
Bread rolls and loaves. More product ranges planned in future. Products and stockist information can be found on the website.

GFF Direct

www.gffdirect.co.uk
Stocks a range of gluten-free products from different manufacturers that can be purchased online.

Glutafin

www.glutafin.co.uk
A range of foods, as well as recipes and information. Products and stockist information can be found on the website.

Gluten Free Foods

www.glutenfree-foods.co.uk
A wide range of Barkat products that can be purchased online. Has been manufacturing gluten-free products since 1994.

Goodness Direct

www.goodnessdirect.co.uk
A wide range of products including many gluten-free ranges, available online. See the 'special diets' section of the website.

Greens Gluten-Free Beers

www.glutenfreebeers.co.uk
A wide range of beers, ales and lagers that can be purchased online.

Hale and Hearty

www.halenhearty.co.uk
A range of more unusual gluten-free products, gluten-free falafel mix, cassava crisps, savoury veggie fritter mix. Products and stockist information can be found on the website.

Hambleton Ales

www.hambletonales.co.uk
Gluten-free ale and lager that can be purchased direct from the company.

Juvela

www.juvela.co.uk

A major provider of gluten-free foods, Juvela offers a complete prescription range of gluten-free alternatives to everyday staples which can also be purchased through pharmacies. Complimentary gluten-free starter pack available.

Lifestyle healthcare

www.gfdiet.com

Vast product range, including ready to roll pastry, crumpets and gluten-free hampers that can be purchased online.

Livwell

www.livwell.eu

Quality bread and cakes. Does a welcome pack for people with coeliac disease. Products and stockist information can be found on the website.

Proceli

www.proceli.co.uk

A wide range of gluten- and wheat-free foods. Products and stockist information can be found on the website.

Rizopia

www.rizopia.com

A wide range of good quality rice pasta. Products and stockist information can be found on the website.

Sally's Sizzlers

www.sallyssizzlers.com

A wide range of gluten-free sausages and other meats that can be purchased online.

Trufree

www.trufree.co.uk
A wide range, particularly good quality crackers and biscuits. Products and stockist information can be found on the website.

Wellfoods

www.wellfoods.co.uk
Bread, rolls and pizza bases. Products and stockist information can be found on the website.

Book List

The Food and Drink Directory
By Coeliac UK, High Wycombe, 2010.

The Gluten-Free Cookbook
By Kyle Cathie, London, 2006.

The Gluten-Free Cookbook for Kids
By Adriana Rabinovich, Random House, London, 2009.

Healthy Gluten-Free Eating
By Darina Allen and Rosemary Kearney, Kyle Cathie Ltd, London, 2009.

Recognition and Assessment of Coeliac Disease
NICE Clinical Guideline 86, 2009.
(Available for free from www.nice.org.uk/CG86)

Seriously Good Gluten-Free Cooking
By Phil Vickery, Kyle Cathie Ltd, London, 2009.

Your Guide to Coeliac Disease,
By Peter Howdle, Hodder Arnold, London, 2007.

Need - 2 - Know

Available Titles Include ...

Allergies A Parent's Guide
ISBN 978-1-86144-064-8 £8.99

Autism A Parent's Guide
ISBN 978-1-86144-069-3 £8.99

Drugs A Parent's Guide
ISBN 978-1-86144-043-3 £8.99

Dyslexia and Other Learning Difficulties
A Parent's Guide   ISBN 978-1-86144-042-6 £8.99

Bullying A Parent's Guide
ISBN 978-1-86144-044-0 £8.99

Epilepsy The Essential Guide
ISBN 978-1-86144-063-1 £8.99

Teenage Pregnancy The Essential Guide
ISBN 978-1-86144-046-4 £8.99

Gap Years The Essential Guide
ISBN 978-1-86144-079-2 £8.99

How to Pass Exams A Parent's Guide
ISBN 978-1-86144-047-1 £8.99

Child Obesity A Parent's Guide
ISBN 978-1-86144-049-5 £8.99

Applying to University The Essential Guide
ISBN 978-1-86144-052-5 £8.99

ADHD The Essential Guide
ISBN 978-1-86144-060-0 £8.99

Student Cookbook - Healthy Eating The Essential Guide
ISBN 978-1-86144-061-7 £8.99

Stress The Essential Guide
ISBN 978-1-86144-054-9 £8.99

Adoption and Fostering A Parent's Guide
ISBN 978-1-86144-056-3 £8.99

Special Educational Needs A Parent's Guide
ISBN 978-1-86144-057-0 £8.99

The Pill An Essential Guide
ISBN 978-1-86144-058-7 £8.99

University A Survival Guide
ISBN 978-1-86144-072-3 £8.99

Diabetes The Essential Guide
ISBN 978-1-86144-059-4 £8.99

View the full range at **www.need2knowbooks.co.uk**. To order our titles, call **01733 898103**, email **sales@n2kbooks.com** or visit the website.

   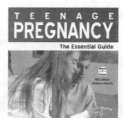 

Need - 2 - Know, Remus House, Coltsfoot Drive, Peterborough, PE2 9JX